Competitiveness

The

United States

in

World Trade

**American Enterprise Institute
for Public Policy Research**

COMPETING IN A CHANGING WORLD ECONOMY

PROTECTING INTELLECTUAL PROPERTY RIGHTS:
ISSUES AND CONTROVERSIES

Robert P. Benko

INVENTIONS IN THE MARKETPLACE:
PATENT LICENSING AND THE U.S. ANTITRUST LAWS

Paul S. Hoff

AUTOMATION TECHNOLOGY AND INDUSTRIAL RENEWAL:
ADJUSTMENT DYNAMICS IN THE U.S. METALWORKING SECTOR

Donald A. Hicks

THE POLITICS OF INDUSTRIAL POLICY

Claude E. Barfield and William A. Schambra, editors

PROTECTIONISM: TRADE POLICY IN DEMOCRATIC SOCIETIES

Jan Tumlir

TRADE IN SERVICES: A CASE FOR OPEN MARKETS

Jonathan David Aronson and Peter F. Cowhey

HIGH-TECHNOLOGY POLICIES: A FIVE-NATION COMPARISON

Richard R. Nelson

THE R&D TAX CREDIT:
ISSUES IN TAX POLICY AND INDUSTRIAL INNOVATION

Kenneth M. Brown, editor

Competitiveness

The

United States

in

World Trade

Sven W. Arndt
and
Lawrence Bouton

American Enterprise Institute for Public Policy Research
Washington, D.C.

We are indebted to Robert Baldwin, Claude Barfield, Lester Davis, Geza Feketekuty, Keith Maskus, and Murray Weidenbaum for valuable comments and suggestions.

S.W.A./L.B.

Distributed by arrangement with
UPA, Inc.
4720 Boston Way
Lanham, MD 20706
3 Henrietta Street
London WC2E 8LU, England

Printed in the United States of America

Contents

5 THE POLICY AGENDA   57

APPENDIXES

LIST OF TABLES

LIST OF FIGURES

1
Introduction

International trade is not an issue that rivets public attention, but it has been pushed into the political limelight by the pronounced and sustained deterioration of the U.S. trade balance and by a general erosion of American competitiveness. It has generated a great deal of activity in the Congress and a series of aggressive trade initiatives in the executive branch. More generally, America's declining strength in international trade has contributed to dissatisfaction with the institutional arrangements governing world commerce and to a loss of confidence in free and open trade.

Among the factors that have brought about this state of affairs, three deserve particular attention. They are macroeconomic policies at home, gradual but fundamental realignments in global competitive conditions, and unfair overseas trade practices exacerbated by weaknesses in multilateral institutional arrangements. Although the fairness issue has tended to dominate recent headlines, the first two causes are by far the more important.

There is no denying the existence and disruptive influence of unfair trade practices. Some countries have been eager to exploit world trade for export purposes but have seen little need to help nurture and preserve the system. Moreover, the rules and institutions governing world commerce, established when trade was dominated by a handful of countries in Europe and North America, are in urgent need of reform, for they do not seem up to the task of managing the frictions and disputes in what has since become a much more complex and diversified world economy.

It would be a mistake, however, to believe that America's competitiveness problems can be resolved simply by making the playing field more level, because the sudden and sharp deterioration in the U.S. trade balance occurred in the absence of a sharp rise in unfair trade practices. Any sharp and influential changes that occurred were in domestic monetary and fiscal policies.

America's trade problems are to a significant extent a result of errors and oversights in the public and the private sectors alike. A major weakness of recent U.S. policy has been a tendency to ignore

1

the exchange rate and balance-of-payments effects of domestic policies, and a major shortcoming of management and labor has been to underestimate the importance of foreign competition.

Although none of these problems is insoluble, the solutions are neither simple nor painless, and the incentives to avoid such solutions in favor of palliatives will be difficult to resist. Fortunately, in the private sector at least, some serious moves toward improving the situation are under way.

These issues are examined in detail in the following pages. Chapter 2 evaluates the contribution of macroeconomic factors to America's trade and exchange rate problems, paying special attention to domestic monetary and fiscal policies. Chapter 3 examines the changing nature of competitiveness around the globe and its implications for the United States. Chapter 4 takes up the issue of unfair trade practices abroad and of weaknesses in multilateral institutions and procedures. A final chapter evaluates the findings and considers the options available to U.S. policy makers. It concludes that America's trade problems are serious but by no means beyond repair, provided that the hard choices needed to improve our situation are faced squarely.

In the short to medium term the major focus must be on restructuring U.S. macroeconomic policies. A large budget deficit combined with a relatively low saving rate makes a large current account deficit unavoidable. If the Congress and the president seriously intend to reduce the trade imbalance, they have no choice but to close the gaping hole in federal finances.

Unfair foreign trade practices are a major irritant to Americans, and justifiably so, but even significant progress in this area will not be enough to compensate for the anticompetitive effects of poor macroeconomic policies. Moreover, significant progress in rewriting the rules and standards governing international trade will inevitably require change in U.S. policies and practices in agriculture, textiles, and other industries.

In the long run the problem of competitiveness is nothing more than preservation of the relative superiority of U.S. capital and labor. Prevailing attitudes and practices, in the private and the public sectors alike, are in many ways incompatible with this task and must be changed. Competitive opportunities are plentiful in industry and in high-value-added services, and those who foresee a nation producing many low-value-added services are wrong, except that their policy prescriptions, if adopted, will become self-fulfilling prophecies.

The greatest danger to America's future as a major world trader comes not from foreign competition, although that presents a formidable challenge. Rather the immediate threat comes from some of the policies under consideration in the political arena.

2

2
Macroeconomic Determinants of Competitiveness

The U.S. trade deficit increased fivefold in the six years beginning in 1980, deteriorating from $36 billion in 1980 to $170 billion in 1986. During the same period the current account moved from a surplus of $1.8 billion to a deficit of $141 billion. Between 1980 and early 1985 the dollar appreciated on a trade-weighted basis by approximately 60 percent. (See appendix D for a discussion of the current account.)

This deterioration of the U.S. trade picture occurred across a wide range of commodities and with respect to most trading partners (as figure 1 shows). If unfair trade practices are to be blamed for this sudden and massive erosion of U.S. competitiveness, a sudden and widespread surge in unfair trade practices must have occurred, but the evidence does not show it. There is similarly no evidence that the gradual changes in world market conditions and in the long-run division of labor suddenly became substantially less gradual in the early 1980s.

One element, however, did change suddenly and massively, and that is the real value of the U.S. dollar, which soared to unprecedented heights (see figure 2). Inasmuch as general exchange rate changes of this kind cannot be brought about by shifts in competitiveness at the industry or even the sectoral level, the causes of the dollar's surge must be sought at the systemwide or macroeconomic level.

The unprecedented appreciation of the dollar during this period has been widely attributed to the rise in U.S. real interest rates relative to rates abroad and to the inflow of capital it provoked, while the trade deficit has been blamed on growth in domestic demand, especially after the recession of 1982. There has been less agreement on the causes of high real interest rates, some analysts blaming anti-inflationary monetary policies, others expansionary fiscal policies, and still others the tax changes contained in the Economic Recovery and Tax Act (ERTA) of 1981.[1]

These disagreements notwithstanding, the appreciation of the dollar is widely acknowledged as the cause of the deterioration of the

FIGURE 1

U.S. Merchandise Trade Balance with Selected Countries
and Regions, 1970–1986
(billions of dollars)

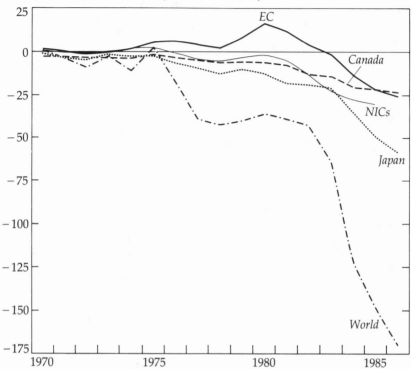

NOTE: The figures for the European Community (EC) include only data for those countries that were members before 1985. The newly industrializing countries (NICs) include Brazil, Hong Kong, Mexico, Singapore, South Korea, and Taiwan.

SOURCES: International Monetary Fund, *Direction of Trade Statistics*; and U.S. Bureau of the Census, *Highlights of the U.S. Export and Import Trade*, FT 990, December 1986.

trade balance and the current account. There is equally widespread conviction that the dollar must depreciate substantially if the trade picture is to be turned around. Consequently, when the dollar depreciated after February 1985 and the trade balance failed to improve, even after allowing for well-known adjustment lags, many observers began to question the efficacy of flexible exchange rates and to look with more favor on the possibilities of international monetary reform.

The evidence suggests that the influences emanating from the real and financial sides of the economy were pushing the exchange

4

FIGURE 2

U.S. MERCHANDISE TRADE BALANCE, CURRENT ACCOUNT, AND REAL EXCHANGE RATE, 1970–1986

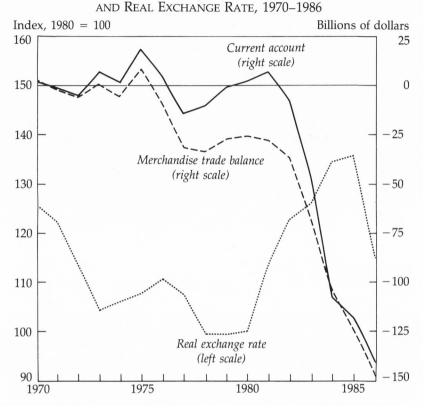

NOTE: The real exchange rate is derived using wholesale prices in the United States relative to a geometric average of wholesale prices in other industrial countries; 1986 figures based on average of first three quarters of 1986.
SOURCE: International Monetary Fund, *International Financial Statistics*.

rate in opposite directions. A surge in demand for imports would normally be expected to lead to depreciation of the dollar, unless, of course, the increased demand for foreign exchange that it created were matched by a rise in supply in some other part of the system, such as a rise in capital inflows due to changed conditions in the financial sector. Under the influence of these conflicting forces, the path of exchange rates would be determined by the dominant influence. It hence appears from the substantial appreciation of the dollar in the 1980s and the known increase in domestic demand that financial influences were dominant.

Does this mean that real and financial influences were due to separate and different disturbances, or may they have been part of the same general disruption of the system? This and related system-wide aspects of the U.S. competitiveness problem are examined in this chapter, after which the discussion turns to sector- and industry-specific concerns.

Determinants of the Current Account

At the economy-wide level, "trade problems" are synonymous with trade balance and current account deficits.[2] Over time the paths of the current account and the trade balance are determined principally by changes in relative prices and in relative incomes. If the prices of a country's products relative to prices abroad rise, exports will shrink while imports expand. Similarly, when a country's incomes relative to incomes abroad rise, the demand for imports tends to rise faster than the demand for exports, and the trade balance deteriorates. If these are the major determinants of the trade balance and the current account, the massive deterioration in those accounts in the early 1980s must have been the result of significant changes in one or both of these variables. We examine each briefly below.

The Real Exchange Rate. If home and foreign prices are to be comparable, they must be expressed in the same currency, so that the prices of, say, import-competing products may be compared with the prices of imports. The comparison may be made in the domestic or the foreign currency, and the choice is one mainly of convenience. The means of moving between the two currencies is the nominal exchange rate, which is the price of one country's money in terms of another's. Hence the dollar price of an import is simply its foreign-currency price multiplied by the dollar price of that country's currency.

How the producer of an import-competing product makes out in such a comparison depends on his own product's price, the foreign price of the imported substitute, and the nominal exchange rate. A change in one of these variables affects his "competitive" strength, but not every change is meaningful, because a change may be nullified by offsetting changes in the other variables. The close interaction among the three variables suggests that changes in, say, the foreign price of imports will be matched, at a given exchange rate, by changes in the prices of import-competing goods, the match becoming more complete as the substitutability between the two product groups increases.

This price comparison may be carried out at various levels of aggregation, and the ratio of domestic prices to foreign prices, made comparable by means of the nominal exchange rate, is the real exchange rate. Three measures of the real value of the dollar—relative export unit values, relative unit labor costs, and relative wholesale prices—are given in figure 3. For each the figure gives the ratio of the domestic price or wage variable, multiplied by the cost to foreigners of the dollar, to the comparable foreign variable. The steep rise after 1980 in the real value of the dollar is reflected in all three measures.[3]

The real exchange rate serves as an approximate measure of a

FIGURE 3

U.S. REAL EXCHANGE RATES, 1970–1986
(index, 1980 = 100)

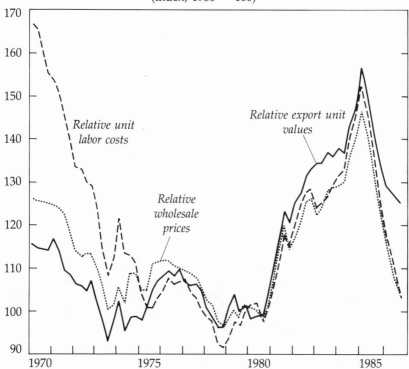

NOTE: The indicators of the real exchange rate represent the ratio of the relevant indicators for the United States to a geometric average of the other industrial countries.
SOURCE: International Monetary Fund, *International Financial Statistics.*

country's international competitiveness. A steep rise implies a decline in competitiveness and, if it persists, an eventual deterioration in the trade balance and the current account. The close correlation between the real exchange rate and the two trade measures is depicted in figure 2.

At the economy-wide level, the real exchange rate expresses competitiveness across all traded goods and with respect to all trading partners. It is therefore an average concept, but it cannot be a straight average, because countries are not all equally important trading partners. Rather, the nominal exchange rate used in competitiveness calculations must be a trade-weighted average, which gives relatively more weight to the dollar's appreciation vis-à-vis the currencies of major trading partners, reducing the weight as a country's importance in U.S. trade declines.[4]

To illustrate the importance of this procedure, compare the depreciation after February 1985 of the dollar in relation to the yen and the German mark with its path vis-à-vis the Canadian dollar (against which it actually appreciated) and the currencies of Taiwan and South Korea (against which it remained relatively stable, as shown in figure 4). Inasmuch as the last three countries are major U.S. trading partners, the dollar's trade-weighted change against all five currencies is substantially less than its bilateral depreciation against the yen or the mark.

This distinction is relevant to trade balance developments after February 1985. Those who focused on the dollar's steep and rapid depreciation against the yen and the mark expected a turnaround in trade that was faster and larger than warranted by the more limited and more gradual depreciation of the dollar on a trade-weighted basis.[5]

Relative Income Growth and the Current Account. The current account is also affected by movements in domestic and foreign incomes. Imports are part of overall expenditure at home and abroad, and overall expenditure depends importantly on income. Thus domestic income growth raises the demand for imports and thereby tends to weaken the current account; income growth abroad raises the demand by foreigners for American exports and thereby strengthens the trade balance.

The relatively rapid recovery of economic activity in the United States after the recession of 1982–1983 no doubt contributed to the deterioration in the trade balance as faster domestic income growth raised imports more than foreign income growth raised exports. When the U.S. economy began to slow down later in the decade, policy makers saw this development as improving the trade balance pro-

FIGURE 4

U.S. Nominal Exchange Rates, 1980–1986
(deviation from 1980)

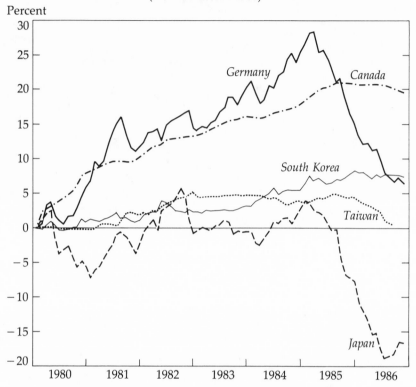

SOURCE: International Monetary Fund, *International Financial Statistics*.

vided that economies abroad continued to grow at adequate rates. U.S. officials took great pains to urge greater policy activism on other governments, especially those of Germany and Japan.

If foreign income growth is an important source of demand for U.S. exports, the austerity programs forced on the less-developed countries by the global debt crisis help explain the sluggish performance of U.S. exports after 1982. As figure 5 clearly shows, the United States suffered a major setback in its trade with indebted developing countries. This setback was due, in no small measure, to the choice of austerity as a principal means of managing the debt crisis. It implies, moreover, that an early resolution of the crisis—or at least a transition from crisis management to long-run adjustment—that would permit

FIGURE 5

U.S. EXPORTS AND IMPORTS WITH SELECTED MAJOR DEBTOR COUNTRIES, 1970–1986
(billions of dollars)

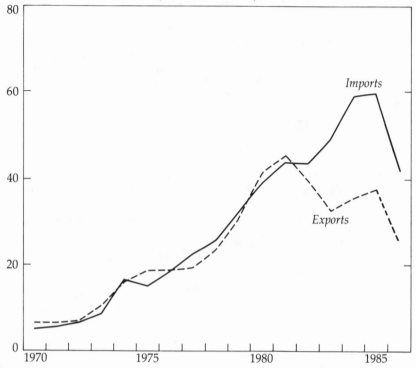

NOTE: Major debtor countries include those countries with outstanding debt estimated at more than $17.0 billion in 1985.
SOURCE: International Monetary Fund, *Direction of Trade Statistics*.

debtor countries to return to higher growth paths should be beneficial to the U.S. trade balance.

If import demand in the United States and in the rest of the world were equally responsive to income growth, equal rates of growth at home and abroad would leave the current account balance unaffected, since U.S. imports, driven by domestic income growth, and U.S. exports, driven by overseas income growth, would expand at the same rate. That symmetry, unfortunately, does not exist. The evidence strongly suggests that income elasticity of demand for imports is higher in the United States than abroad.[6] Hence equiproportionate income growth at home and abroad tends to worsen the U.S. trade balance, so that, in the absence of other influences, real depreciation of the dollar would have to accompany symmetrical income growth to prevent the U.S. current account from deteriorating.

The Current Account: The Mirror of the Macroeconomy

We have noted the important correlation between movements in relative prices and in relative incomes and the paths of the trade balance and the current account. It is tempting to view price and income movements as causes and trade balance changes as effects, because that causal chain accurately describes many modern balance-of-payments episodes. But even where exchange rate changes are responsible for trade balance developments, the means by which those exchange rate changes are brought about determine the influence of exchange rates on the trade balance.

This is important because the current account is part of the larger economy and hence cannot be changed without appropriate changes in the rest of the economy. A current account surplus is after all the excess of domestic output over domestic absorption—by means of consumption, investment, and government expenditures—of goods and services. A current account deficit reflects an excess of domestic absorption over output, describing an economy that consumes more than it produces. Hence changing the current account means changing the balance between domestic output and absorption of goods and services.

When a country runs a current account surplus, it sells more goods and services abroad than it buys and accumulates the difference in claims on the future output of other countries. This is net foreign investment. The United States did exactly that for most of the postwar period, building up an impressive international investment position (see table 1). It used that accumulated wealth to finance the large current account deficits of the 1980s. In roughly half a decade, the United States used up an international creditor position that had taken several decades to build.

Nothing is intrinsically wrong with such a saving-dissaving cycle, because for countries as for individuals one purpose of accumulating wealth is to smooth fluctuations in income and output relative to absorption. These fluctuations will normally not be synchronized among countries, so that the ability of one country to run a current account deficit is limited by the willingness of others to run surpluses. Without a Japan, a Germany, and several other creditor countries, the United States could not have supported private and public sector activities in the 1980s by means of net imports from abroad and would have

TABLE 1

INTERNATIONAL INVESTMENT POSITION OF THE UNITED STATES,
1980–1985
(billions of dollars; year-end)

Type of Investment	1980	1981	1982	1983	1984	1985[a]
Net international investment position of the United States	106	141	136	89	4	−107
U.S. assets abroad	607	720	825	874	898	952
U.S. government assets	90	99	108	113	120	131
U.S. private assets	517	621	717	761	779	822
Direct investment abroad	215	228	208	207	213	233
Foreign assets in the United States	501	579	689	786	894	1060
Foreign official assets	176	180	189	195	199	202
Other foreign assets	325	399	500	591	695	858
Direct investment in the United States	83	109	125	137	165	183

a. Preliminary.
SOURCE: U.S. Department of Commerce, Bureau of Economic Analysis, *Survey of Current Business* (June 1986), p. 28, table 2.

been forced instead either to forgo them or to crowd out other activities.

Indeed, in the absence of trade a country's absorption in each period is limited by its output for that period. If more resources are demanded in the public sector, say, through expansion of the government deficit, private consumption and investment must be curtailed and crowded out.[7] In the presence of international trade, however, the current account offers an additional source of resources, so that a surge in government demand relative to revenues need not lead to an equal amount of internal crowding out.

To the extent, however, that a sudden increase in net imports reflects a surge in domestic absorption relative to output, the deterioration in the current account can only be reversed by reversing that surge. These are the considerations behind the conclusion that if the government deficit was responsible for the growth of net imports in the 1980s, only reduction in that deficit (as a percentage of gross national product) or crowding out of an equivalent amount of private expenditures can bring lasting improvements in the U.S. trade picture.

The correlation between financial balances in the private and public sectors and the current account is depicted in figure 6. It sug-

FIGURE 6

U.S. PRIVATE SECTOR BALANCE, GENERAL GOVERNMENT
BUDGET DEFICIT, AND CURRENT ACCOUNT, 1973–1985
(percentage of gross domestic product)

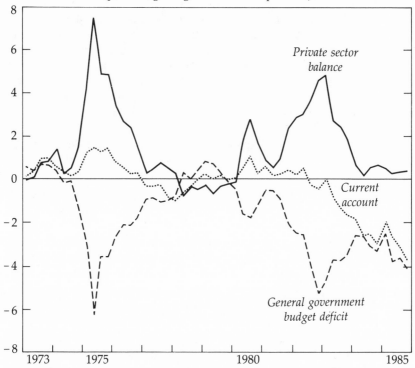

NOTE: The private sector balance is the difference between private gross savings and private gross investment. The general government budget deficit is the sum of the federal, state, and local governments' budget deficits. See appendix B for more details.
SOURCE: U.S. Department of Commerce, *National Income and Product Accounts.*

gests that current account improvements must await better balance between private and public demand and total domestic output.[8]

For policy makers the message is that measures aimed at improving the current account that do not improve the internal balance between output and absorption will not work. In considering policy initiatives such as import surcharges, exchange market intervention, target zones, and economic stimulation by other countries, the key question to be kept in mind is whether and to what extent such policies are capable of correcting the underlying imbalance between output

13

and absorption in the U.S. economy.

Needless to say, if all creditor countries around the globe simultaneously decided that they had accumulated enough dollar assets and elected to raise their own domestic absorption relative to output, the source of U.S. net imports would dry up, and the U.S. current account would have to improve at a pace determined by the shrinking collective surplus of our trading partners. If, as is likely, the federal deficit remained relatively unaffected by such changes, the shrinking supply of outside resources would require larger portions of the government deficit to be financed through private domestic crowding out. Interest rates would rise, and interest-sensitive rather than exchange-rate-sensitive sectors and industries would bear a rising share of the burden.

That would be the outcome if all our creditors reduced their lending to us and hence their current account surpluses. If only one or two countries did so (along the lines urged upon Japan by the United States), the effect on the U.S. current account would be mainly to alter its country composition rather than to reduce its size.

It is not unreasonable to ask, given the stress in the foregoing discussion on the balance between domestic absorption and output, why U.S. output did not keep better pace with expanding U.S. demand, especially in light of the presence of unemployment and excess capacity throughout the economy. Indeed, it was the surge in net imports in the face of sectoral unemployment that convinced many that trade was the cause of American joblessness.

The answer lies in part in the uneven nature of the expansion and the greater boost it gave to demand for nontradables than to demand for tradables. The budget-led expansion raised demand for nontradables—in construction, services, defense, and government— and hence necessitated a reallocation of productive resources away from tradables (mining, agriculture, and much of manufacturing), where net imports could bridge any emerging imbalances between demand and supply. If relative wages, capital rentals, and other resource prices were sufficiently flexible and labor, capital, and land sufficiently mobile between the two sectors, such a reallocation of resources and such a restructuring of activities would have been accomplished without much friction and hence without much loss in employment and capacity utilization.

Adjustments of this sort are never easy, however, especially in the short run, not even in the relatively flexible U.S. economy. Hence demand soared and factor prices rose in the domestic sector, where many new jobs were created, while relatively immobile resources stagnated in the tradables sector. Some wage reduction did occur

14

through wage give-backs and the like, wage growth slowed substantially, and land prices and capital rentals plummeted in agriculture and elsewhere in the tradables sector. But these changes did not go far enough in light of the substantial change in underlying macroeconomic conditions, and so the erosion of competitiveness could not be prevented. The outcome forced much of the burden of adjustment on exchange-rate-sensitive sectors and industries of the U.S. economy.

The Role of Financial Markets and Capital Movements

The current account deterioration was necessitated by the sharp rise in domestic demand relative to output. If financial markets around the world were imperfectly integrated and capital relatively immobile internationally, such a major surge in domestic demand and hence in net import demand could not be financed abroad quite so readily, and hence interest rates at home would have to rise more to free domestic financial resources for use in the public sector. Further, the additional foreign exchange demanded to finance net imports would not be readily forthcoming, so that currency depreciation would be needed to ration foreign exchange. Both developments would tend to dampen the force of the recovery.

In the 1980s, however, financial markets were highly integrated, capital was internationally mobile, and the debt crisis and other global uncertainties made dollar assets look especially secure and attractive to resident and foreigner alike. As interest rates in the United States relative to rates abroad rose, American investors stayed home, and foreigners showed themselves more than eager to buy a piece of the action. Capital flowed in great abundance and helped lift the dollar to unprecedented heights.

The Relative Importance of Monetary and Fiscal Policies

There has been considerable debate over the relative roles of the Federal Reserve's anti-inflationary monetary policy and the government's fiscal and tax policies in the exchange rate and balance-of-payments developments of the early 1980s. When financial markets are integrated, an anti-inflationary monetary policy tends to exert two influences on interest rates. The reduction in liquidity tends to raise both nominal and real interest rates, while the control and reduction of inflationary expectations tend to lower nominal interest rates and to raise real rates. In the early 1980s nominal interest rates fell in the United States while real rates rose (as figures 7 through 10 show).

15

FIGURE 7

NOMINAL SHORT-TERM INTEREST RATES, FIVE NATIONS, 1970–1986
(percent)

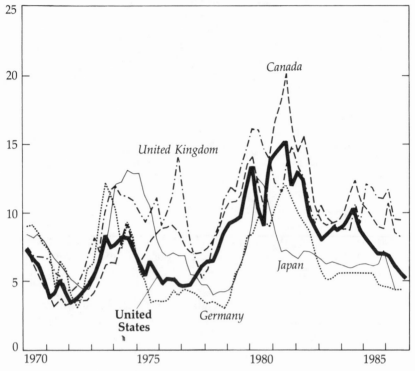

SOURCE: International Monetary Fund, *International Financial Statistics*.

These developments suggest that the expectations effects of Federal Reserve policies dominated the liquidity effect, permitting nominal interest rates to decline. Real rates would, of course, be expected to rise under pressure from both liquidity and expectations effects.[9]

At the same time, an anti-inflationary monetary policy tends to raise the nominal value of the dollar along the lines described in the preceding section. The effect of this kind of monetary policy on the real exchange rate is more ambiguous and depends on the specifics of structural adjustment rigidities and expectational considerations. It is hence unlikely that monetary policy alone could have produced the large and sustained real appreciation of the 1980s. The force behind that appreciation must be sought elsewhere.

Fiscal expansion financed by debt issue tends, other things being

FIGURE 8

REAL SHORT-TERM INTEREST RATES, FIVE NATIONS, 1970–1986
(percent)

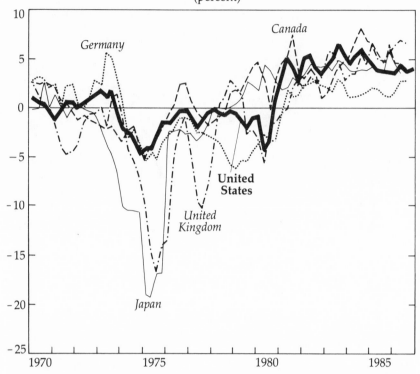

NOTE: Nominal short-term interest rates are deflated by changes in the consumer price index averaged over the previous quarter, the current quarter, and the next quarter to obtain the real interest rate.
SOURCE: International Monetary Fund, *International Financial Statistics.*

the same, to raise domestic nominal and real interest rates. Other things are not, of course, always the same. The evidence shows, for example, that the extent of excess capacity makes a difference, as does the willingness of foreigners to lend.[10]

The effect of a debt-financed fiscal expansion on the real exchange rate is to appreciate the currency, especially if the increase in domestic demand falls disproportionately on domestic rather than internationally traded goods. In that event domestic productive resources must be shifted from tradables-producing to nontradables sectors of the economy. One way to bring about this redeployment is for the prices of nontradables to rise in relation to the prices of tradables, and one

FIGURE 9

NOMINAL LONG-TERM INTEREST RATES, FIVE NATIONS, 1970–1986
(percent)

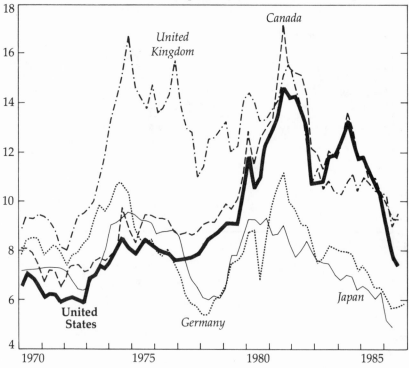

SOURCE: International Monetary Fund, *International Financial Statistics*.

way to accomplish this relative price change is by means of currency appreciation.[11]

The relative price of tradables fell dramatically in the early 1980s, as figure 11 makes clear, underscoring the magnitude of the shift in economic signals produced by government policies during that period. The United States created many new jobs at that time, the majority of them in the domestic area; but for relatively sector-specific resources in tradables production—labor, capital, and land—with limited mobility, the period was one of relative and sometimes absolute stagnation.

These considerations suggest that the principal cause of relative stagnation in the tradables sector of the U.S. economy was not the trade deficit, as some observers have claimed, but the unbalanced

FIGURE 10

REAL LONG-TERM INTEREST RATES, FIVE NATIONS, 1970–1986
(percent)

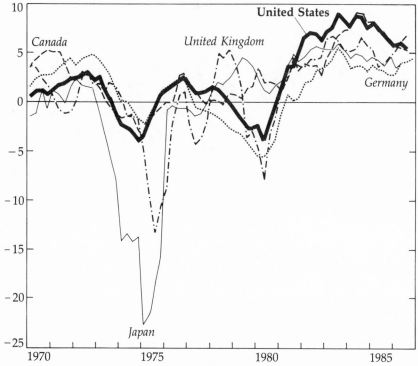

NOTE: Nominal long-term interest rates are deflated by changes in the consumer price index averaged over the previous quarter, the current quarter, and the next quarter to obtain the real interest rate.
SOURCE: International Monetary Fund, *International Financial Statistics*.

nature of the domestic expansion and the pressures it put on domestic resource deployment. The only way to increase the supply of nontradables is to increase domestic output, but an excess demand for tradables can always be supplied by imports. Hence, if the required surge in output was to be forthcoming, capacity in the nontradables sector needed to be augmented. The additional resources could be entirely new—new investment, new entrants into the labor force, and so on—or redeployed from tradables production. But to achieve this shift in resources, prices, wages, and other factor rewards had to rise more in nontradables than in tradables. Inevitably, some prices

FIGURE 11

U.S. Relative Prices, Tradables versus Nontradables,
1970–1985
(1972 = 100)

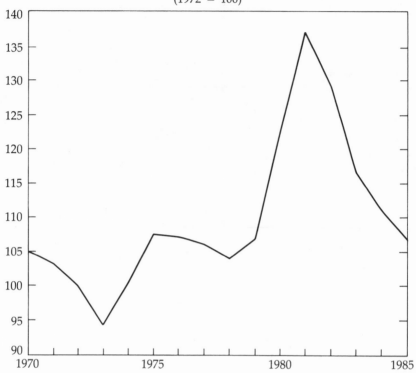

NOTE: Tradables include manufacturing and mining industries; nontradables include all other industries. Tradable and nontradable prices are obtained by the sum of component industry price levels weighted by GNP figures.
SOURCES: Authors' calculations based on Department of Commerce, *National Income and Product Accounts*.

and factor rewards were sticky, and relative changes would meet resistance. In addition, some resources were sector-specific—agricultural land, as well as some labor and capital in manufacturing. In combination, wage stickiness and immobility could lead to unemployment in these circumstances. Employment and high capacity utilization could be maintained only with requisite reductions in factor prices. Overall, however, the U.S. economy reacted with remarkable flexibility and resilience to what was by all measures a massive wrenching of the signals of economic policy.

Implications for Future Policy

The deterioration of the trade balance in the early 1980s was sudden and sharp. Such a large and sustained change can be caused only by an equally sharp change elsewhere in the system. Of the three principal causes to which the U.S. competitiveness problem has been attributed, only the macroeconomic explanation meets the condition of a sharp, sudden, and discontinuous change; neither of the two others—unfair foreign trade practices and fundamental changes in global competitiveness—experienced the pronounced shifts needed to provoke the observed trade balance deterioration.

This deterioration reflected the more rapid growth in U.S. demand for goods and services than in output; and output failed to keep up with demand partly because of the heavy concentration of new demand that fell on nontradables. To bring about the redeployment of domestic resources that would provide the additional output of nontradables, the relative price of the latter had to rise and that of tradables to fall. Dollar appreciation accomplished that result, but in the process the burden of adjusting to the budget deficit and the rise in domestic absorption that it set in motion fell heavily on exchange-rate-sensitive industries.

This finding suggests that the principal solution to the U.S. trade problem must come in the area of macroeconomic policy. This point is by no means fully understood in the Congress, judging from the trade bill passed by the House of Representatives in 1986 and from various other proposals circulating in the Congress. Some proposals would place surcharges on imports in general; others would penalize imports from countries with large bilateral trade surpluses. The problem with such efforts is that they are likely to hurt U.S. exporters directly by raising costs relative to costs abroad. They imply negative effective protection for exporters. If, moreover, such policies do not correct the underlying imbalance between domestic demand and output, their effect on the current account will be minimal. The dollar may actually appreciate in real terms if such policies fail to alter the sectoral distribution—between goods that are and those that are not traded internationally—of domestic demand.

The pressures in the Congress to do something are considerable, but a viable solution of the budget deficit problem has thus far eluded both the Congress and the executive branch. Moreover, the relative sluggishness of the world economy now raises concerns that budget balancing in the United States could unleash a global recession—hence the urgency with which U.S. officials are pressing other countries to stimulate their economies so as to give the United States room for fiscal retrenchment.[12]

21

One way, however, for the United States to make room and provide incentives for overseas expansion is to correct macroeconomic imbalances at home. A budget-reducing policy combined with actions that restored better sectoral balance to domestic demand would contribute to real depreciation of the dollar and would thus provide relief from pressures on competitiveness without necessarily stifling U.S. growth and the U.S. demand for imports.[13]

In this respect current official U.S. policy regarding the global debt problem is in need of review. Far more must be undertaken—more even than the germ of an idea contained in the Baker initiative of 1985—to permit debtor countries to shed austerity in favor of faster economic growth.

Notes

1. See, for example, *Economic Report of the President* (Washington, D.C., February 1985), p. 105; Martin Feldstein, "Domestic Saving and International Capital Movements in the Long Run and the Short Run," *European Economic Review* (Amsterdam), vol. 21 (March/April 1983); Martin Feldstein and C. Horioka, "Domestic Saving and International Capital Flows," *Economic Journal* (London), vol. 90 (June 1980); and Alessandro Penati and Michael Dooley, "Current Account Imbalances and Capital Formation in Industrial Countries, 1949–1981," *IMF Staff Papers*, vol. 31, no. 1 (March 1984), pp. 1–24. See also M. Hutchison and C. Pigott, "Real and Financial Linkages in the Macro-economic Response to Budget Deficits: An Empirical Investigation," in Sven W. Arndt and J. D. Richardson, eds., *Real-Financial Linkages among Open Economies* (Cambridge, Mass.: MIT Press, forthcoming 1987).

2. For more detail on the various definitions of "trade balance," see appendix D, "How Many Trade Balances Are There?"

3. There is often much confusion over the terminology used to describe movements in exchange rates. A depreciation or devaluation indicates a decrease in the value of a currency in terms of other currencies (that is, more dollars are required to purchase a unit of foreign currency). An appreciation or revaluation indicates the opposite, an increase in the value of a currency (that is, fewer dollars are required to purchase a unit of foreign currency). Devaluation and revaluation are concepts used in connection with a system of fixed exchange rates, where the government changes the value of a currency by decree, while depreciation and appreciation refer to exchange rate changes under floating rates, brought about by market forces.

4. The effective exchange rate compiled by the International Monetary Fund is an index combining the exchange rates of eighteen industrial countries with weights derived from the IMF's multilateral exchange rate model (MERM). The weights are estimated from the model in such a way that they take into account the size of trade flows as well as the relevant price elasticities and the feedback effects of exchange rate changes on domestic costs and prices. The IMF's MERM rate has been criticized because of the limited choice of

industrial countries used in the model and because of the way in which the weights are constructed. The group of countries used excludes many of a country's major trading partners. The issue with regard to the weights centers on the choice of multilateral versus bilateral construction. For fuller discussion of these issues, see Jeffrey A. Rosensweig, "A New Dollar Index: Capturing a More Global Perspective," in the Atlanta Federal Reserve Bank's *Economic Review* (April 1986); W. Michael Cox, "A New Alternative Trade-weighted Dollar Exchange Rate Index," in the Dallas Federal Reserve Bank's *Economic Review* (September 1986); and Morgan Guaranty Trust Company's *World Financial Markets* (July and August 1983).

5. Appendix C examines real exchange rate changes with respect to specific countries and commodities.

6. The income elasticity of imports measures the responsiveness of imports to changes in domestic income. For a fuller discussion of price and income effects on trade, see Morris Goldstein and Mohsin S. Khan, "Income and Price Effects in Foreign Trade," in Ronald W. Jones and Peter B. Kenen, eds., *Handbook of International Economics* (Amsterdam: North-Holland, 1984), vol. 2. Examples of income elasticities collected in that study are presented in the following table.

ESTIMATES OF INCOME ELASTICITIES FOR TOTAL IMPORTS

	Estimates							
Country	A	B	C	D	E	F	G	Average
Canada	1.20	1.18	n.a.	0.95	0.90	n.a.	1.87	1.22
France	1.66	1.30	1.28	1.45	1.32	1.57	1.07	1.38
Germany	1.85	1.35	1.52	1.17	1.34	1.42	1.46	1.44
Japan	1.23	1.12	1.30	1.26	0.93	0.77	1.69	1.19
United Kingdom	1.45	1.24	1.78	1.46	1.07	2.24	2.57	1.69
United States	1.68	1.81	1.84	1.89	0.76	1.53	4.03	1.93

n.a. = not available.
A = H. S. Houthakker and F. P. Magee, "Income and Price Elasticities in World Trade," *Review of Economics and Statistics*, vol. 51 (May 1969).
B = G. B. Taplin, "A Model of World Trade," in R. J. Ball, ed., *The International Linkage of National Economic Models* (Amsterdam: North-Holland, 1973).
C = M. Goldstein and M. S. Khan, "Large versus Small Price Changes and the Demand for Imports," *IMF Staff Reports*, vol. 23 (March 1976).
D = L. Samuelson, *A New Model of World Trade*, OECD Occasional Studies (Paris: OECD, 1973).
E = F. G. Adams et al., *An Econometric Analysis of International Trade* (Paris: OECD, 1969).
F = V. J. Geraci and W. Prewo, "An Empirical Demand and Supply Model of Multilateral Trade," unpublished paper, University of Texas, March 1980).

G = J. F. Wilson and W. Takacs, "Differential Responses to Price and Exchange Rate Influences," in "Foreign Trade of Selected Industrial Countries," *Review of Economics and Statistics,* vol. 61 (May (1979).
NOTE: The table shows by what percentage total imports will increase with a 1 percent rise in income.
SOURCE: Goldstein and Khan, "Income and Price Effects."

7. In a closed economy the crowding out of private expenditure through increases in the cost of credit is the principal means of making room for a government deficit. Appendix B develops these interrelationships in greater detail.

8. This relationship and the relative movements of private sector saving and investment and the combined deficit of all levels of government are shown in the table on the facing page.

9. These and other aspects of macroeconomic and exchange rate policies are examined in greater detail in Sven W. Arndt, "The Exchange Rate, International Monetary Arrangements, and Competitiveness," American Enterprise Institute, January 1987.

10. The interest rate effect of fiscal expansion was a major point of disagreement between the Reagan administration and its critics; even within the administration some blamed the deficit, but others blamed changes in the tax treatment of investment contained in the Economic Recovery and Tax Act of 1981 for the increase in real interest rates. The administration officially noted that empirical studies were mixed on the relation between fiscal deficits and interest rates. And since the contemporary wisdom saw the rise in real interest rates as the cause of the dollar's appreciation, this empirical uncertainty weakened the connection between the budget deficit and the exchange rate. Further, since the conventional wisdom saw the real currency appreciation as the essential cause of trade balance deterioration, the administration concluded that the link between the fiscal deficit and the trade deficit had also been exaggerated.

11. Indeed, the real exchange rate is sometimes defined as the ratio of the price of tradables to that of nontradables. For details, see Arndt, "Exchange Rate."

12. In 1985 Germany imported goods worth $158.5 billion from the rest of the world. Imports from the United States constituted about 7 percent of the total. Thus, for every 1 percent increase in German income, German imports will increase 1.44 percent, or $2.3 billion. If the United States maintained its share in the German market, it could expect its exports to Germany to increase $0.2 billion for every 1 percent increase in German income.

13. If these alternatives are rejected for fear of unleashing world recession, trade measures of the sort proposed and contemplated in the Congress are inappropriate as well, because they will hurt foreign production.

NET SAVINGS AND INVESTMENT, 1951–1985
(percentage of GDP)

| | Private Sector Balance | | | General Government Savings | | Domestic Savings-Investment Balance | Balance of Payments on Current Account |
| | Personal savings | Business savings | Domestic investment | State and local surplus (+) or deficit (−) | Federal surplus (+) or deficit (−) | | |
Year	A +	B −	C +	D +	E	= (A+B−C+D+E) =	F
1951–60	4.7	2.4	6.5	−0.2	−0.2	0.3	0.2
1961–70	4.7	3.2	7.0	0.1	−0.5	0.5	0.5
1971–80	4.9	2.1	6.1	0.9	−1.9	0.0	0.0
1981	4.6	1.4	4.8	1.3	−2.2	0.4	0.2
1982	4.4	1.0	1.8	1.1	−4.8	−0.2	−0.3
1983	3.6	2.3	2.8	1.3	−5.4	−1.0	−1.3
1984	4.3	3.1	6.6	1.4	−4.8	−2.6	−2.8
1985	3.2	3.2	5.8	1.5	−4.9	−2.8	−3.0

SOURCE: U.S. Department of Commerce, *National Income and Product Accounts of the United States.*

3

The Changing World Economy

Inasmuch as macroeconomic policies have had a major influence on recent setbacks in U.S. trade and competitiveness, straightening out those policies must be given a primary role in any effort to turn the situation around, at least at the economy-wide level. There can be little question that U.S. macroeconomic policies in the 1980s have severely damaged the tradables sector and that policy makers in the future will have to pay far more attention to the effects of their "domestic" policies on exchange rates and the balance of payments.

Although better macroeconomic policies should help improve the competitive position of the U.S. tradables sector, they are by no means the solution to all of America's trade problems. The nature of global competition is changing in a process that has already brought difficulties to a number of U.S. industries and that will, as it unfolds, challenge many another industry in the United States and in other industrial countries. It is thus crucial that Americans—policy makers as well as private citizens—clearly understand the altered nature of the environment in which they must compete.

In a sense U.S. attitudes toward global competition are still dominated by successes achieved during the "American era" of the first quarter-century after World War II. The world, however, is a very different place now and changing rapidly before our eyes. It is different not so much in what determines competitiveness as in the nature of the competition and in the United States as competitor. In understanding and dealing with this situation, two common pitfalls must be avoided. First, it is not correct that all of America's trade difficulties are due to unfair foreign trade practices. Although unfair and unneighborly practices are a serious problem, very much in need of urgent attention, their elimination will not save every American industry, let alone every producer operating in the tradables sector.[1]

A fallacy at the other extreme is to make comparisons between the current situation and the era of American economic hegemony to measure the extent of the country's decline. The United States began the postwar era in a position of unrivaled economic supremacy as the major competition in Europe lay either vanquished or exhausted. The United States was the supplier of last resort and hence dominated world markets more than basic considerations of comparative advantage would have permitted in more normal times.

Hence comparisons with market shares in years before Europe's reconstruction and recovery give unrealistic and biased results that overstate the magnitude of the U.S. decline.[2] Moreover, comparison of market shares as a measure of trade performance is subject to another bias, this one inherent in the causes and the nature of recent growth in the world economy.

In much of the postwar period, world income has grown faster than income in the United States, a phenomenon that is not surprising in light of the low levels from which many countries started. During this period world trade has grown still faster, so that a diminution in the U.S. share of world exports and imports in general and in a variety of manufacturing activities should not be cause for alarm.

These considerations make trade performance tests based on changes in market shares tricky business to be handled with care and circumspection. Ideally, cost comparisons at various levels of disaggregation are needed for proper estimation of competitiveness and comparative advantage, but systematic and reliable cost data are rarely available, especially as the degree of disaggregation rises.

This is not to say that information on U.S. competitiveness is entirely lacking. The major factors determining competitiveness are relatively well established and have not changed very much, as recent U.S. experience confirms. In the broadest terms, competitiveness in trade is still strongly related to relative resource abundance, especially where specialization among countries takes place at the industry level and where trade possesses a strong interindustry character. This kind of trade is especially important between industrial and newly industrializing countries and with less-developed countries. When it comes to trade among similar economies, as in Europe and in the Atlantic community, where trade has a pronounced intraindustry character, economies of scale and product differentiation, as well as technology gaps created by research and development (R&D), are important.

Two major developments in the postwar era have fundamentally altered the competitive game to the disadvantage of the established and mature industrial economies in Europe and North America. One is the emergence of new and highly aggressive competitors, beginning with Japan and continuing with the newly industrializing countries of Asia and Latin America. Not infrequently their competitive challenges were encouraged by the magnitude of economic rents earned by productive factors in established industries. The other is the quick-

27

ening pace of international communication and the more rapid diffusion of information and technical knowledge it has engendered.

This means that competitive advantage conferred by advances in technical knowledge, in product design, and in process innovation is less durable and more fleeting. The shrinking length of the technology gap and the contraction of the product cycle create competitive challenges for advanced industrial countries quite apart from problems associated with piracy of intellectual property, because there is less time to recoup the costs of innovative activity and greater pressure for further advances.

The effects of these factors on the composition of U.S. trade, on value added in manufacturing, and on employment in manufacturing are captured in figures 12, 13, and 14. U.S. manufactures are divided into three categories: (1) resource-intensive products (including lumber and forest products and processed and semiprocessed raw materials), also known as Ricardo goods after David Ricardo, the nineteenth-century British economist; (2) standardized commodities, produced according to well-established and widely available design criteria and for equally well-established uses by means of common technologies (including carbon steels but not specialty steels, ordinary textiles and apparel but not designer textiles or the more specialized industrial fabrics, and standard memory chips but not custom chips, gate arrays, or logic chips), also known as Heckscher-Ohlin (H-O) goods, after two Scandinavian economists who first studied their importance; and (3) product-cycle goods, which are broadly the opposite of Heckscher-Ohlin goods, namely, specialized rather than standardized, new rather than mature, with potential uses and applications still unexplored, with new and not yet well-established production technologies, and generally requiring significant inputs of R&D and human capital (engineers, scientists, design artists, marketing specialists, and so on.).[3]

The figures not only provide important insights into recent U.S. trade experience but broadly confirm general theoretical expectations. Note, first, the decline in all three measures of the trade balance after 1980, underscoring the widespread influence of the appreciation of the dollar in the early 1980s. Consider next the longer-run trends inherent in each curve, with product-cycle goods generating a consistent and rising trade surplus and Ricardo goods a gently worsening trade deficit while the trade balance in H-O goods shifts from a small surplus in the 1960s to a deficit that widens, gradually at first and then increasingly precipitously.

Value added (as a percentage of total value added in manufacturing) tells a similar story, with product-cycle goods on a rising trend and Ricardo goods relatively unimportant and holding more or less

28

FIGURE 12

U.S. TRADE BALANCE FOR RICARDO GOODS, PRODUCT-CYCLE GOODS, AND HECKSCHER-OHLIN GOODS, 1958–1985
(billions of dollars)

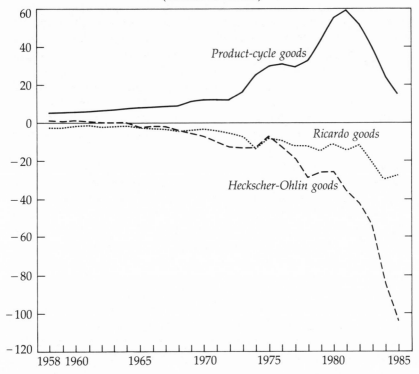

NOTE: For definitions of kinds of goods, see text.
SOURCES: Authors' calculations based on data from the U.S. Department of Commerce, Office of Business Analysis, 1985 Industrial Outlook Data Computer Tape; and Bureau of Census, Foreign Trade Division, Reports EA 675 and IA 275. The classification of three-digit SIC industries into product-cycle, Ricardo, and Heckscher-Ohlin goods comes from Keith E. Maskus, "The Changing Relationship between Basic Inputs and U.S. Foreign Trade," Competing in a Changing World Economy Project, Working Paper no. 2 (Washington, D.C.: American Enterprise Institute, August 1985).

steady while H-O goods play a strongly dominant role at 45 to 50 percent of total manufacturing in the 1960s and then begin a significant decline in the 1970s. This experience is mirrored by employment (as a percentage of total employment in manufacturing), where the overall stability of the employment share of H-O goods is noteworthy,

FIGURE 13

U.S. VALUE ADDED IN RICARDO GOODS, PRODUCT-CYCLE GOODS,
AND HECKSCHER-OHLIN GOODS, 1958–1985
(percentage of manufacturing)

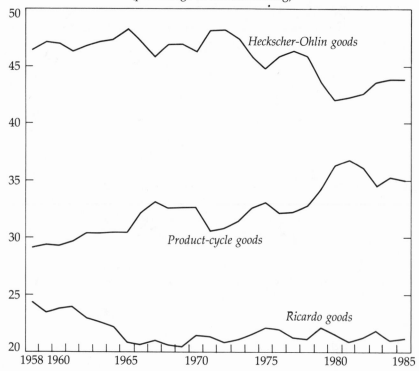

NOTE: For definitions of kinds of goods, see text.
SOURCES: Same as figure 12.

in spite of the decline of the late 1970s and early 1980s. These considerations affect the outlook for U.S. competitiveness in the years to come.

Resource Endowments

Its relative abundance of arable land is bound to give the United States a continued competitive edge in agriculture, but our own policies and restrictive practices abroad becloud the outlook for agricultural production and trade. Prospects depend ultimately on the coming round

FIGURE 14

U.S. TOTAL EMPLOYMENT IN RICARDO GOODS, PRODUCT-CYCLE
GOODS, AND HECKSCHER-OHLIN GOODS, 1958–1985
(percentage of manufacturing)

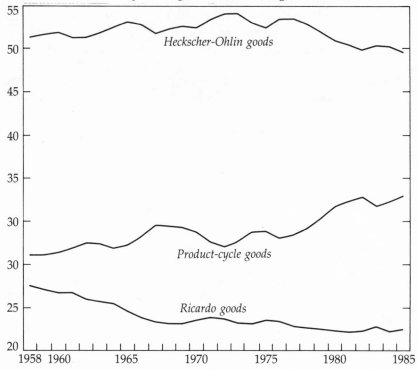

NOTE: For definitions of kinds of goods, see text.
SOURCES: Same as figure 12.

of the General Agreement on Tariffs and Trade (GATT) and the extent
to which it succeeds in rationalizing not only agricultural trade but
domestic agricultural policies in the United States, the European Community, Japan, and the developing countries.[4] Among resource-intensive industries, the outlook is mixed, with forest products relatively
well off and copper under heavy pressure.

The United States continues to be relatively abundant in capital
and skill and should thus continue to enjoy competitive advantage
in products making intensive use of physical and human capital. In
both respects, however, the picture is less clear cut than it once was,

because the U.S. abundance of capital and skill, though still overwhelming in absolute terms, is declining relatively as other countries accumulate capital and develop human skills faster than the United States (see table 2).

The global distribution of productive resources is changing in response to demographic factors, differential rates of capital accumulation, the spread of technical know-how, and differences in educational practices. Government policies, institutional arrangements, and cultural attitudes play an important role in the preservation and enrichment of a nation's endowment of productive resources. In a dynamic world economy no nation can take for granted its position in the international division of labor, but the United States may have done just that.

The fact that other countries are accumulating capital and skill faster is not entirely surprising in light of the low levels from which

TABLE 2

SHARES OF WORLD RESOURCES, SELECTED COUNTRIES, 1963 AND 1975
(percent)

Country	Year	Capital	Skilled Labor	Semiskilled Labor	Unskilled Labor	Arable Land
United	1963	41.93	29.36	18.27	0.60	27.44
States	1975	33.43	26.33	19.09	0.18	29.25
Japan	1963	7.09	7.84	12.56	0.30	0.90
	1975	14.74	8.62	12.33	0.25	0.78
United	1963	5.60	6.97	6.48	0.14	1.13
Kingdom	1975	4.89	6.44	5.32	0.07	0.98
West	1963	9.12	7.08	6.79	0.14	1.29
Germany	1975	8.27	6.56	5.79	0.08	1.13
Korea	1963	0.13	0.57	1.75	1.39	0.33
	1975	0.40	0.75	2.07	1.71	0.34
Hong	1963	0.08	0.21	0.27	0.19	0.00
Kong	1975	0.12	0.19	0.38	0.09	0.00
Argentina	1963	1.29	1.73	1.98	0.43	4.36
	1975	1.27	1.57	2.93	0.40	4.83
Mexico	1963	1.07	1.64	2.17	2.06	3.86
	1975	1.59	2.12	2.99	1.44	3.91

SOURCE: Harry P. Bowen, "Changes in the International Distribution of Resources and Their Impact on U.S. Comparative Advantage," *Review of Economics and Statistics*, vol. 65 (August 1983), p. 405.

most countries start. It nevertheless diminishes the U.S. share of the world's stock of capital and skilled labor (and would raise the U.S. share of the global stock of less skilled labor except for rapid population growth in many poor countries).

As capital and skilled labor become more abundant in other countries, their need to obtain the products of capital and skilled labor through trade with the United States is reduced, and domestic production replaces imports. As this process unfolds, some countries may become exporters as well, bringing export competition and import penetration in product areas that are today still considered the preserve of advanced countries. Skilled workers in the United States must thus expect mounting competitive challenges in the future.

The change in global distribution of productive resources is confirmed in a recent study by Harry P. Bowen, who finds that in the 1970s the growth of capital per worker in the United States was one of the lowest in a sample of thirty-four countries and that, as a result, the United States slipped from first place in 1967 to sixth place in 1975 in capital per worker. Ranked near the top (in accumulation of capital) were South Korea, Japan, and several developing countries.[5]

In a similar evaluation Bowen finds the U.S. rate of accumulation of skilled labor also among the lowest, so that the country's rank in the ratio of skilled to total labor slipped from second place in 1963 to seventh in 1975. Bowen's research suggests further that, after rising in the 1960s, the capital and skill content of U.S. exports declined, especially in trade with developed countries.

The implications are straightforward: as capital accumulation continues abroad, foreign producers will mount challenges in capital-intensive products, much as they have done in labor-intensive products. The challenges come initially in capital-intensive standardized products, that is, H-O products, and have already brought distress to some heavy industries; they then spread to other markets.

Improvements in labor skills abroad, always relatively speaking, enable foreign workers to challenge Americans with similar skills in an increasingly wide range of skill-intensive products. The answer for American management and labor lies in staying ahead of the game, and the product-cycle good offers the major opportunity for doing so.

The Product Cycle

The quickening pace of innovation and of imitation, the latter made possible by the greater speed with which knowledge and information are disseminated around the globe, is shortening the life cycles of many products. Some products mature and become standardized faster, others are replicated faster, and in either case the competitive advantages that accrue to the innovator are eroded faster than in the past.

Although this phenomenon has been widely noted, it seems not to have affected behavior very much. Blue-collar workers, in particular, tend to think of lifetime work in terms of a narrow range of tasks, supported by relatively little training, much of it acquired in youth and through learning by doing. Labor unions devote considerable resources and energies toward defining, securing, and then defending specific tasks. Inflexibility is the hallmark of this approach. It is uncommon in this environment to view skills as human capital that needs to be improved and upgraded from time to time to free its owner from attachment to given tasks, jobs, and firms and to provide flexibility and occupational mobility. In other words, too much emphasis is placed on enhancing earnings through the creation of economic rents and too little on enhancing them by investing in human capital and improving skill. The former, unfortunately, contributes to inflexibility.

The fault, however, lies not merely with workers, who would not find it easy, under existing capital market and institutional arrangements, to locate lenders willing to finance investment in improving human capital. A long-run solution to this problem must go beyond the educational system and include capital market structure. This problem has substantial public policy dimensions, because well-known externalities limit privately financed on-the-job-training.

What has been said about rigidity, immobility, and job-specific skills among workers can be said about the design of factories and other physical capital, about the management of inventory or working capital, and about investment in the quality of production processes. Fortunately, existing institutional arrangements, including financial market structure, constitute less of an obstacle to improvements in this area, and accumulating evidence suggests that important steps are being taken at the initiative of the private sector. The shortening product cycle and the quickening pace of global competition require more flexibility and greater ability to adjust than were needed in the more tranquil past.

Creating Comparative Advantage

It is clear from this chapter's discussion that comparative advantage and competitiveness are dynamic rather than static and can be influenced by policy, because policy can influence the accumulation of productive resources. Capital and human capital are created resources, and a nation's competitive position is thus determined in part by its relative success in creating resources. Public policy plays a major role in this process, through education, job training, tax and subsidy programs, defense department expenditures, and more. But in recent years the idea has been advanced that these activities are inadequately coordinated and insufficiently focused on creating competitiveness. This has been the main criticism of many supporters of industrial policy.

The idea has been inspired to a significant extent by the widespread perception that it explains Japan's strong international competitive position. Japan's industrial might is widely believed to have been created by an omniscient, forward-looking, dynamic Ministry of International Trade and Industry (MITI), which guided and directed the deployment of resources and the creation of comparative advantage. The role of MITI has been greatly exaggerated, at least in the popular mind.[6] The focus on MITI has deemphasized other important contributing factors, such as labor-management relations, high saving rates, extraordinary productivity growth, and so forth. Some attributes are cultural, some conditions were created independently or perhaps even in spite of MITI, but some were doubtless catalyzed by MITI.

Although the Japanese experience may need reinterpretation and may not be transferable to other countries in its entirety, the notion of active policy management of comparative advantage should not be dismissed lightly. It has generated particularly lively discussion in the context of high technology, where many observers believe that the United States cannot maintain competitiveness without active government participation.

The essential case for government intervention must be made on grounds of market failure: that without the aid of government private markets and private firms will not support certain activities that contribute to comparative advantage. Those market failures might be due to externalities, diseconomies, and the like, and the purpose of public policy is to correct and overcome them. R&D is widely believed to suffer from such problems.

The case does not rest on the failure of private decision makers to see opportunities that are obvious to politicians and bureaucrats. Rather, it rests on differences between private and public costs and benefits, so that perfectly rational calculations render certain activities economically infeasible from the private perspective yet highly desirable from the point of view of society at large. Differences of this sort may be due to differences in risk and uncertainty as perceived by the individual firm and as relevant to society, or they may be due to differences in benefits. The problem may be quickly illustrated in terms of differences between private and public benefits.

A private firm measures the benefits of R&D expenditures by the returns that accrue to that firm, while the total benefit from society's perspective includes benefits derived by others in addition to those who financed it. A private firm's willingness to spend on R&D declines as the likelihood rises that others will copy the results of its research and thereby prevent it from fully appropriating the returns. This decision, though rational from the firm's perspective, is undesirable from the general point of view, because the benefit to society does not depend directly on which firm or how many firms exploit the idea and benefit from it.

Piracy of intellectual property is the international version of this problem. Private firms in advanced countries may cut back R&D expenditures in response to piracy (through patent and copyright violations). Job training and human capital formation more generally may suffer similar undersupply if firms financing them expect newly trained workers to be hired away by competitors. Such a decision may be quite rational from the individual firm's perspective but may nevertheless be undesirable from society's point of view, because the benefits associated with a more skilled work force do not depend directly on where it is employed. This is perceived as less of a problem in Japan, where workers' loyalty is greater and more extensive job training by firms may hence be justifiable.

These considerations suggest that inasmuch as comparative advantage is influenced by resource abundance and by technological superiority, failure of private firms to provide adequate supplies of skills and technological advance for the perfectly rational reasons given above will prevent a country from fully exploiting the potentials of dynamic comparative advantage. Hence government intervention may be required to generate the socially optimal rate of growth of comparative advantage.

This makes the case in principle for government intervention. It rests not on the superior ability of bureaucrats to see the future or on the inherent narrow-mindedness of private decision makers but on a difference in returns as viewed from private and public perspectives. The theoretical case is straightforward, but implementation is not. Serious operational difficulties arise when legislatures and public institutions seek to identify the industries where market failures of this kind are a problem, and they arise in the formulation of policies that must seek to correct existing distortions without creating new ones.

The evidence is not reassuring in this respect. There is at least as much evidence that governments (including MITI) will get their industrial policy decisions wrong as that they will get them right, particularly as the focus of those policies narrows and becomes more specific. No systematic evidence suggests that governments will err less than private decision makers. Steel, shipbuilding, textiles, telecommunications, automobiles, and aircraft are examples, and the list goes on. The record simply is not very encouraging when it comes to policies on specific industries, products, or firms, suggesting that government intervention is best focused on economy-wide infrastructure problems and their role in capital formation, R&D, and human resource management.

The reasons for this poor record are not hard to find. Nor should they be surprising, because as intervention becomes more specific to particular industries or firms, policy makers become more exposed to the conflicting claims of the private interests directly involved and the larger public interest. Rather than correcting a narrowness of private decision making, policy becomes hostage to narrow private interest, thereby violating the very principle that justified intervention in the first place.

Policy failure is often due to a poor choice of instruments, so that intervention creates new distortions in the process of trying to correct existing distortions between private and public costs and benefits. This is especially relevant to the use of trade policy as an instrument of intervention. If the problem is an inadequate private supply of R&D expenditures or of privately financed job training, the subsidization of such activities is a more efficient means of raising supply than trade policy (for reasons that are discussed in detail in the appendix to this chapter "Competitiveness and Comparative Advantage"). If workers cannot obtain private financing for human capital investment and unexploited social benefits from such investment exist, domestic policies—including financial market regulation—are superior to trade policies, not least because the latter mainly protect existing jobs. In such cases outright subsidies, including temporary income maintenance schemes, tend, according to the available evidence, to be less costly than protection. Direct domestic policies of this sort are also more transparent, enabling voters to form a clearer picture of what is being done at what cost.

Protection of infant industries has a long history and has been justified on grounds that entry into global markets dominated by large established firms may be difficult in the presence of economies of scale. Private operators may not be able to carry the early losses during the period when production is less than optimal despite the clear prospect of long-run competitiveness for the domestic industry. One reason may be that domestic securities markets value short-run realized returns more than long-run expected returns, given the discount factors at work. Another may be differences between private and social expected benefits, for the reasons discussed above.

In such a case the divergence of private from social expected returns justifies intervention in principle, but the optimal policy is still a domestic policy such as a subsidy, especially if the infant industry tariff raises the price of the product to domestic users. An infant industry tariff is less efficient but has been justified for use especially by less-developed countries whose fiscal systems are also less developed and hence not always capable of supporting domestic tax-subsidy schemes.

Japan is widely perceived as having used access-restricting trade policies to build its industrial strength. To the extent that Japan was in a catch-up position and underdeveloped when it began the process, industrial support may have been justified on infant industry grounds, leaving the question whether trade restrictions or domestic subsidies were the more efficient tool. The United States had recourse to the infant industry tariff to develop its pharmaceuticals industry in the face of powerful competition from established firms in Switzerland and Germany.

An essential condition of the infant industry case for industry support and tariff protection is the explicitly terminal nature of that support. Support is to last until the infant has matured to a size that captures the economies of scale and masters the learning curve to be self-supporting. Some Japanese industries may be overdue for graduation.

In sum, the case for managing comparative advantage needs to be evaluated carefully. It is relatively easy to make the case in principle, far more difficult to identify situations requiring intervention, and extremely difficult to design and implement policies that do less harm than good. This is especially true of intervention in specific industries or products, when governments in democratic societies have great difficulty withholding support from the inefficient members of an industry.

Long-Run Employment Prospects

In the continuing debate over trade policy, protectionists have complained that foreign competition is destroying American jobs. Alternatively, they have complained that foreign competition is threatening American wages. These complaints give expression to an inherent long-run conflict or trade-off between preservation of jobs and preservation of incomes and living standards.

The relative abundance of labor in poor countries makes it a relatively inexpensive factor of production there. High-wage workers in advanced countries can compete effectively provided that productivity differences keep pace with wage differences. Hence productivity growth is essential to maintaining competitiveness at high relative wages.

Productivity growth means, however, that a given market share of output can be produced by a smaller number of workers. Employment must fall over time under these pressures, with released workers needing to be redeployed to other employment. The ease with which such adjustment is accomplished depends on growth in labor-absorbing industries. If growth elsewhere in the economy, including other tradables industries and nontradables, is adequate (as it tended to be in the 1950s and 1960s), adjustment will be smooth and protectionist sentiment subdued and localized. When economic growth in the rest of the economy is sluggish (as it tended to be in the 1970s) or when macroeconomic policies distort relative prices and increase the rate of labor shedding in tradables (as they did in the 1980s), adjustment will be painful, and protectionist pressures will surge.

The loss of employment in traditional industries has been blamed by protectionists on trade and changes in sectoral trade balances brought about by foreign competition. The evidence, however, does not support that claim. Indeed, even in textiles empirical studies suggest that of the three factors determining employment changes—productivity growth, demand changes, and foreign competition—productivity changes are the dominant influence.[7] This result is plausible given that the growth in wages and living standards that has taken place in such industries over time has been achieved by means of productivity growth and that, in the absence of huge surges in demand, such gains inevitably come at the expense of employment. If the evidence is correct, it implies that trade policy can do little to arrest the decline in employment in textiles and other industries under pressure and that efforts to save jobs will be exceedingly costly.

Problems of Adjustment

U.S. producers cannot expect to win every competitive battle or preserve every job. If they did, poorer countries would have no hopes of improving their lot. When competitiveness is lost, the question is less what to do about it than how to manage the necessary adjustment. It is not a long-run policy option to prop up uncompetitive firms and industries and maintain them artificially. The costs and the implications for the health of the U.S. economy simply do not permit it.

This constraint is widely understood and accepted, but the possibilities of temporary aid and adjustment assistance still exist. Temporary aid may be justified if without it adjustment would occur in a manner or at speeds that would be too disruptive and disorderly from society's perspective or would create sudden and unacceptable changes in income distribution.

In such cases, however, governments have been prone to two types of policy mistakes that have tended to be very costly. The first relates to the difficulty of ensuring that relief will be temporary and will facilitate rather than impede adjustment. The protection and relief granted the textile and apparel industries for well nigh two decades are examples of policies that began, in the United States and other industrial countries, as temporary but have become enshrined in permanent institutions such as the Multi-Fibre Arrangement (MFA).

Such policies are also basically unneighborly in that they achieve a domestic goal of income redistribution—from textile user to producer—at the expense of foreigners. The textile arrangement is an especially black mark against the advanced countries since it denies poorer countries a chance to improve their living standards in what is often the only area in which they possess comparative advantage; it puts in question our commitment to the principle of free and open trade.

A second policy error arises in connection with the choice of policy instrument once a decision to intervene has been made. When the problem to be rectified is of domestic origin, whether it is due to distortions and imperfections in domestic production or consumption or to intolerable inequities in domestic income distribution, trade policy is relatively inefficient and hence inappropriate, because it tends to create new distortions and imperfections. In general, domestic policies—including tax, subsidy, and regulatory policies—are more efficient means of achieving such objectives (as discussed in more detail in the appendix to this chapter "Policy and Market Distortions"). They are also more transparent and hence enable politicians and voters better to evaluate policy choices and their effectiveness.

These considerations are relevant to the much-discussed issue of trade adjustment assistance, which may be justified in principle if unassisted and uncontrolled adjustment is too fast and too disorderly or too slow and if it carries with it undesirable distributional changes. But if the poor quality of adjustment is due to market imperfections and if they are not confined to markets of importables, all those affected by them should be eligible for assistance. Hence the tendency for existing assistance programs to be limited to trade-related adjustment makes little sense. Moreover, if the weaknesses in adjustment are due to imperfections in domestic markets—in information, training, housing, transportation, and so on—corrective policies that aim directly at the imperfections are superior to trade policy. Several proposals currently circulating would use revenues raised from import surcharges or user fees or from auctioning of existing quotas and other quantitative restraints to finance adjustment assistance.[8]

That adjustment will be difficult and resisted is to be expected, given the localized incidence of the burden of adjustment compared with the widespread distribution of the benefits from efficient trade and specialization. The costs and benefits of adjustment as calculated by individual workers, firms, and communities are bound to differ substantially from the costs and benefits that are relevant to society, especially in view of the presence of substantial economic rents. When wages and the returns to other inputs exceed their opportunity costs because of the presence of economic rents, workers, capitalists, and the communities whose tax bases they support have powerful incentives to resist relocation and its tendency to destroy rents.

In such cases a lump-sum adjustment subsidy may very well be needed to bring social and private costs and benefits of adjustment into better balance and thereby facilitate the kind of adjustment that is socially desirable. From the perspective of society as a whole, such subsidies coupled with market-determined relocation will in the long run be cheaper than protracted trade intervention and its tendency to delay adjustment and hence to raise costs.

The severity of adjustment problems and consequent protectionist pressures may depend on whether changes in competitiveness are intraindustry rather than interindustry. This is so because in the former the factor intensities of contracting and expanding activities are similar and hence skill requirements are more likely to be similar. Adjustment is easier because the retraining and the industrial restructuring needed are less extensive. Under such circumstances workers may more justifiably pursue narrow skill specialization and companies focus on narrower product specialization.[9]

When changes are interindustry, however, and foreign countries limit access to their own markets while pushing exports, adjustment is more difficult in that it tends to require more substantial retraining and retooling and more elaborate and costly changes in specialization. This forces firms and workers to be more diversified and flexible.

In the first phase of the postwar period, growth in trade took place mainly among the countries of the Atlantic community, and its dominant element was an expansion of intraindustry trade. Adjustment was comparatively easy, and trade liberalization was widely supported. The arrival of Japan and of the Asian newly industrializing countries changed the pattern of trade expansion. By pursuing export-led growth while rigidly restricting access to their own markets, they prevented adjustment from following an intraindustry pattern. If their markets had been more open, the surge of their exports and the growth in incomes it brought would have created new opportunities for exports from the advanced countries. A pattern of growth and expansion might have developed in which, say, Japan's imports of the products of a broadly defined industry would have grown along ` with its exports of products in that industry. Instead we see a sustained rise in Japan's manufacturing exports while imports lag. The newly industrializing countries have, of course, chosen to follow the Japanese example.

Conclusion

We conclude this chapter by taking note once again of changes in the conditions of global competition. These changes are taking place against a background of rapid and differential accumulations of capital and human capital around the world, accumulations that are changing not only the total world supply of capital and skilled labor but their distribution among countries. In this process the U.S. share of the world stock of capital and human capital is declining, and its decline has inevitable effects on the distribution of comparative advantage. These evolving changes in the international division of labor obtain additional impetus from a wider and more rapid diffusion of information and technological knowledge.

The most severe competitive challenges have come in light, labor-intensive manufactures (including textiles and apparel) and in capital-intensive heavy industry. The products in question have tended to be standardized in design, in production technology, and in application and have been easily replicated. High-wage workers in advanced countries can maintain their competitive position only with the help of productivity advances, but productivity growth enables a given U.S. market share of output to be supplied by a smaller number of workers. Indeed, productivity growth appears to have been the major source of employment losses, even in the textile industry.

As import-competing sectors shed labor, the rest of the economy must expand so as to absorb labor and thereby contain protectionist pressures. This process is facilitated when overall growth is high and when trade changes are intraindustry or involve activities with similar factor intensities. These conditions appear to have obtained in the 1950s and 1960s but not in the 1970s, when economic growth was less buoyant and trade changes involved activities with less similar factor intensities, or in the 1980s, when domestic macroeconomic policies significantly distorted relative prices and thereby increased the rate at which the tradables sector was shedding labor.

While U.S. trade performance has experienced setbacks in standardized labor- and capital-intensive products, evidence of continued competitive strength abounds in trade of product-cycle goods, where a relative abundance of skilled labor and technological knowledge is sustaining strong competitive advantage. This evidence provides a powerful counterargument to the assertion that Americans are doomed to become low-quality service workers.

The importance of dynamic comparative advantage and the role of relative resource accumulation and relative technological advances in shaping it have given rise to the suggestion that public policy is needed to drive improvements in comparative advantage, especially at the high-technology end of international competition. The economic case for intervention hinges on the presence of market failure, of discrepancies between the private and social costs of such key activities as R&D. Where such discrepancies exist, private markets may undersupply R&D, job training, investment in human capital, and industrial adjustment itself, and the purpose of public policy would be to correct such market distortions and generate socially desirable levels of activities.

Implementing such policies is a major problem, however, especially when they become industry- or even product- and firm-specific. Governments and their agencies, including Japan's MITI, are prone to make two types of costly policy errors. One is a failure properly to establish the location and nature of a distortion; the other is a tendency to costly and inefficient intervention with inappropriate instruments. Among the most frequently abused and misused instruments is trade policy. Intervention tends to be more effective when it is broadly based and environmental.

Appendix: Competitiveness and Comparative Advantage

The Sources of Competitiveness. Specialization and exchange are at the heart of international economic relations and, like most things economic, generate benefits as well as costs. The benefits are the additional national income and wealth that can be produced by a given endowment of national resources through the greater allocative efficiency brought about by specialization. Even a large nation with abundant resources like the United States is not equally efficient in all things and hence derives benefits from specialization and trade. The costs arise from the greater dependence on other countries that

43

accompanies specialization and from the need to adjust the deployment of resources to shifts and changes in the conditions of trade. Efficient specialization should proceed in the direction of comparative advantage or relative competitiveness to ensure that domestic resources are deployed in their most productive uses. The objective is to avoid producing goods that would absorb more resources than the exports needed to obtain them from abroad.

When markets are competitive and technological know-how is comparable among trading partners, resource endowments play a crucial role in determining comparative advantage and hence specialization and trade. In the absence of perfect competition, however, externalities, economies of scale, and other forms of market distortion, as well as differences among countries in technical knowledge, emerge as important additional determinants of competitiveness and help explain the preponderance of intraindustry trade among industrial countries. Even where endowments dominate trade patterns, moreover, changes in relative resource abundance among countries bring about changes in comparative advantage.

Endowments are variable because land, labor, and capital can be created or destroyed. Capital may be accumulated or may decay, population grows and declines, and skills are learned and forgotten. Agricultural land can be claimed from forest, desert, and sea or lost to erosion and urbanization. Changes in the global composition and distribution of resources and widespread dissemination of technology, as well as advances in technology, make comparative advantage and competitiveness dynamic and subject to change. Such changes bring opportunities as well as challenges.

The Relevance of Comparative Advantage. According to received trade theory, it is comparative rather than absolute advantage that should govern specialization and exchange in international trade. Hence even a country that can produce everything at less cost than its competitors gains from specializing in those products in which it has comparative advantage, that is, the greatest cost advantage, leaving other products to be imported. This rule ensures that fewer of the nation's resources will be used up by trade than by direct home production, and it is after all the cost in home rather than foreign resources that is the relevant measure of competitiveness. Thus, if home production requires certain resources and the resource content of exports used to obtain the same product abroad is lower, it should not be produced at home even when the absolute costs are less at home than abroad.

It is the opportunity cost of the home resources given up for a product, whether produced at home or imported, that matters, not whether the nation needs fewer resources to produce it than other countries. In this sense an industrial strategy that is biased against imports is likely to waste national resources and to reduce the rate at which living standards may grow. Moreover, producing at home what would take fewer resources to acquire abroad is unneighborly in that it prevents a country's trading partners from fully exploiting their comparative advantage.

Appendix: Policy and Market Distortions

The Role of Policy. When competition is strong and markets function perfectly, the resulting deployment of resources will be as efficient as possible. Government cannot, in competitive circumstances, improve on the efficiency of economic arrangements and hence cannot redeploy resources in a way that would increase national income and wealth. Indeed, all rearrangements reduce national income, and any rearrangement that makes someone better off necessarily comes at the expense of someone else.

When the private and public costs and benefits associated with economic activities are coincident, the prices and costs that guide private consumption and production decisions reflect the underlying social opportunity costs. In such an environment private maximizing behavior brings about socially optimal results and thereby makes governmental corrective measures unnecessary. With efficiency criteria fully satisfied, the only reason for policy intervention would be on grounds of income distribution.

Real world economies are, of course, far from perfect, and many markets are subject to distortions and imperfections that destroy the coincidence between social and private costs and benefits. Hence the prices and costs on which private economic decisions are based do not always accurately reflect the underlying social opportunity costs. This leads markets to overestimate or underestimate the opportunity costs (that is, the next best alternative uses to which resources may be put) and thus to undersupply or oversupply the products in question. If, in such circumstances, ways could be found to bring private costs and benefits into conformity with social costs and benefits, national income and wealth could be increased.

The traditional model of international trade is based on the assumption of perfect competition. In its Heckscher-Ohlin version it also assumes given resource endowments and uniform technologies among trading partners. Its analytical focus, moreover, is on the nation-state and the effects on national income and wealth of alternative trade regimes. It is not concerned with the distributional effects, assuming that the political process will find ways of resolving distributional disputes by means of appropriate tax or subsidy policies.

These features of traditional trade theory and their apparent inconsistencies with the real world have been criticized in recent years; but in condemning traditional trade theory, critics have often advocated policy remedies that had no logical structure and very uncertain prospects. A common fallacy has been to conclude from the assumptions of the traditional trade model that its results could not be relevant to real world situations and to use that inference as license for large-scale policy intervention designed to override market mechanisms.

Still, the possibility that real world departures from the theory's ideals may significantly alter the policy conclusions should not be dismissed lightly. Policy intervention may, indeed, be needed to correct or offset market distortions and thereby improve market performance. Intervention may also be needed in situations where costs are highly concentrated among the few while benefits are dispersed among the many. These issues and criticisms are important enough to warrant close examination.

The Sources of Market Distortions. Imperfect markets are markets in which the cost-benefit calculations on which private agents base their investment, saving, production, and work and leisure decisions diverge from underlying opportunity costs. This divergence leads to inefficient resource allocations, since it is the opportunity costs and benefits associated with alternative uses of scarce resources that matter from society's perspective.

Imperfections are the result, for example, of externalities, of public goods, and of economies of scale. Consider the classic illustrative case of an industry that in the process of production emits pollutants into the environment. Those affected by this pollution bear the costs of dealing with its effects. The industry's standard supply calculations do not take account of the costs imposed on others by pollution. Those additional costs raise actual costs above those recognized by the industry, and since consumers of the industry's product will be charged a price that covers the industry's costs only, output will be excessive. A tax—on sales or production—or an environmental regulation that holds the industry responsible for maintaining the quality of the environment would raise the industry's costs to the level of society's total costs and move demand and output back to a level at which the price covers all costs.

An analogous case can be made for beneficial externalities in which social cost is less than private cost or social benefit is greater than the benefit obtained by those who pay for an activity. Examples include R&D expenditures that produce knowledge usable by third parties and job training inside a firm that benefits other firms through workers' mobility. In each case the firm undertaking the activity cannot appropriate all the benefits; it will equate its costs with the benefits accruing directly to it and hence supply an amount of the activity that will be too small from society's perspective. A subsidy is then capable of encouraging private suppliers to expand output.

An extreme form of externality in consumption is that of a public good, that is, a good whose total availability rather than the amount owned by an individual provides individual satisfaction. National defense is an example of such a good, which markets have difficulty in pricing and hence tend to undersupply.

It is apparent that policy intervention that succeeds in restoring the coincidence between private and public costs and benefits makes resource allocation more efficient. Intervention often falls far short of its goal, however, partly because governments and bureaucracies do not always fully understand the nature of a distortion, partly because they do not always possess appropriate instruments for dealing with it, and partly because abuses and misapplications are not easy to prevent. Hence policy often adds distortions rather than eliminates them; this applies to tax and subsidy policies, price policies of the sort used in agriculture, minimum wage laws, and regulatory requirements. Most economies are significantly distorted not merely because of market failures but because of policy failures.

The defense argument is one frequently used to justify trade policy. It was used recently to justify U.S. protection of the machine tools industry by means of voluntary export restraints forced on foreign suppliers. It is used by several European countries to justify protection of high-technology and service industries; and it is used by Japan, in its variant of national food security, to protect domestic agriculture. Each country readily justifies its own national security needs while denouncing those of others.

An argument for protection often invoked by developing countries—and used by the United States in the past—is the infant industry argument, according to which new industries require protection from imports to generate economies of scale at which comparative advantage may be achieved. Although infant industry protection is not always easy to justify, it is widely accepted as legitimate. Less-developed countries take this position with respect to trade in services, arguing that proposed liberalization prevents them from building industries with eventual comparative advantage.

When distortions are present, not every intervention is unneighborly. Taxes, subsidies, administrative guidelines, and regulatory restraints may be needed to correct distortions, so that countries conducting such policies cannot be accused of unfair or anticompetitive practices until the conditions surrounding each intervention have been examined. The problem for the trading community of nations is to find appropriate guidelines and standards for policy intervention and surveillance. The work within the GATT on subsidy codes is a step in the right direction.

When distortions are domestic, policies that attack the root of the distortion directly have the greatest likelihood of success. That means tax and subsidy policies rather than trade policies because the latter tend to create new distortions even if they correct existing ones. In case, for example, of a distortion in production, a production tax or subsidy works directly on the affected side of the market while leaving consumption decisions undisturbed, whereas a tariff introduces a distortion in consumption.

Critics of liberal trade claim that "strategic" trade intervention is an effective device for the exploitation of scale economies and is needed in industries that are oligopolistically organized on a global basis. Although recent theoretical work has shown that such policies can raise welfare, the results are highly sensitive to assumptions about the structure of industry, the stability of government policy, and the likelihood of retaliation. Little empirical work has yet been undertaken to test the theory. It is thus premature to suggest that the existing wisdom has been superseded and that the existing system requires fundamental reform. Democratic governments find it difficult to single out some industries and some firms for special treatment that is denied to others.

Notes

1. Unfair trade practices and the means of dealing with them are the subject of the next chapter.

2. For details, see William H. Branson, "The Myth of De-industrialization," *Regulation* (September/October 1983).

3. The classification of SIC industries into Ricardo, Heckscher-Ohlin, and product-cycle goods was based on a paper by Keith Maskus, "The Changing Relationship between Basic Inputs and U.S. Foreign Trade," AEI Occasional Papers, Competing in a Changing World Economy Project Working Paper No. 2, August 1985. Ricardo goods include SIC categories 20, 21 less 214, 24 less 245, 26 less 264 and 265, 29, 311, 313, 324, 325, 327, 328, 333, 335, 336, and 339. Heckscher-Ohlin goods include SIC categories 22, 23, 25, 26 less 261 and 262 and 263, 27, 284, 285, 30 less 304, 31 less 311 and 313, 321, 322, 323, 326, 329, 331, 332, 339, 34, 363, 365, 369, 37 less 372 and 376, and 39. Product-

cycle goods include SIC categories 28 less 284 and 285, 35, 36 less 363 and 365 and 369, and 38.

4. For a detailed analysis of world agriculture, see Sven W. Arndt and Timothy E. Josling, "Issues and Options of U.S. Agricultural Trade Policy: An Overview," AEI Occasional Papers, Competing in a Changing World Economy Project Working Paper No. 1, August 1985.

5. Harry P. Bowen, "Changes in the International Distribution of Resources and Their Impact on U.S. Comparative Advantage," *Review of Economics and Statistics*, vol. 65 (August 1983), p. 405.

6. See, for example, Paul R. Krugman, "Targeted Industrial Policies: Theory and Evidence," in *Industrial Change and Public Policy*, a symposium sponsored by the Federal Reserve Bank of Kansas City, August 24–26, 1983.

7. David Greenaway, *Trade Policy and the New Protectionism* (New York: St. Martin's Press, 1983).

8. Such proposals include a "user fee" proposed by Senator William Roth of Delaware and quota-auctioning schemes proposed in Robert Z. Lawrence and Robert E. Litan, *Saving Free Trade* (Washington, D.C.: Brookings Institution, 1986).

9. Care must be taken, however, not to equate similarities in factor intensities with intraindustry trade.

4

Unfair Trade Practices and Trading System Failures

Fairness has become a major theme of the contemporary trade policy debate. American politicians and labor leaders, as well as many in the business community, bemoan the unfair and anticompetitive practices of our trading partners and the generally unsatisfactory state of the trading order and its principal institution, the General Agreement on Tariffs and Trade (GATT).

This sense of dissatisfaction, long localized in traditional industries like footwear, textiles, steel, and machine tools, has spread to agriculture and many branches of manufacturing, including the high-technology sector, as the dollar has appreciated and the trade balance has deteriorated. As we have already noted, the dollar's appreciation was due mainly to a deterioration in macroeconomic policies—especially in the United States—rather than to a sudden rise in unfair trade practices. We have also noted that some U.S. producers, especially of more traditional products, are faced with a long-run erosion of competitiveness brought on by fundamental changes in the international division of labor.

It seems appropriate in light of the multiplicity of forces at work to ask how important unfair foreign practices and system failures have been in bringing about America's current difficulties in trade and competitiveness. Although a comprehensive and precise answer to the question is not available, we estimate that full compliance, for example, by Japan with U.S. fair trade requests would bring improvements on the order of $5 to $7 billion in a $50 billion bilateral U.S.-Japanese trade deficit (1985 basis), suggesting that unfair trade is minor in comparison with the problems created for U.S. producers by domestic policy makers and by continuing changes in the world economy. It would be a mistake, indeed, if American politicians succeeded in distracting the public's attention from the important problems that need attention and that cannot be resolved by suggesting that an easy and painless solution can be extracted from foreigners.

The Nature of the Problem

Where the fairness of the trading order is concerned, Americans have three major complaints. First are foreign practices restricting market access, including variable levies on agricultural imports into the European Community and administrative guidelines, customs procedures, and technical standards relating to a broad range of imports into Japan. Second are production and export credits, as well as industrial and agricultural dumping, designed to obtain for foreign exporters unfair trading advantages and to support import penetration of the U.S. market and export competition in third markets. Third are shortcomings in the trading system in general and in the GATT in particular, including trade in agriculture and in services, intellectual property rights, subsidies and foreign investment, and dispute settlement procedures.

Unfair Practices Related to U.S. Exports

The United States has accused Japan of using a diversity of nontariff barriers to limit market access. There is little doubt that such practices exist, but what is to be done about them? The United States has tried a variety of unilateral and bilateral offensives, including threats of retaliation and bilateral negotiations, among them the market-opening, sector-specific (MOSS) talks. The ideal solution is the retaliatory threat that succeeds, and for a large country like the United States such threats have a reasonable chance of succeeding. A threat that works is ideal in that it brings benefits to U.S. exporters without damaging the rest of the economy. Note, however, that a significant increase in export sales following an opening of foreign markets will affect the rest of the economy. The redirection of domestic resources into export production is likely to increase imports.

A threat of retaliation that does not work, however, may have to be followed by actual retaliation, and that typically carries costs. Retaliation is often biased against innocent third parties because suitable commodities against which to retaliate are not always available. Retaliatory import restrictions tend, moreover, to raise domestic prices and thereby either reduce consumer welfare or raise costs in domestic and other tradables industries.[1]

Since, as a rule, the imports available for retaliatory restriction will not match the U.S. exports that are denied foreign access, policy makers face difficult political choices of which group of Americans to disadvantage in order to improve the overseas sales of another group of Americans. The recent exchange of trade restrictions with Canada is a perfect example of unproductive trade warfare. Such actions are rarely based on careful cost-benefit considerations and enhance the national welfare only by accident.

Since retaliation of this kind is usually aimed at a particular country, that country may attempt to circumvent the restrictions by trans-shipping its exports through third countries, as the U.S. experience with textiles and apparel has shown. This suggests that, wherever possible, coordinated retaliation among all countries affected by a particular trading partner's restrictive practices may be more effective.

It is partly because unilateral retaliation offers such limited prospects, even to a large country like the United States, that bilateral negotiations have played such an important role. The United States has negotiated with Japan on a wide range of products, some of those discussions occurring in the MOSS talks. Products have included citrus, beef, and plywood, as well as telecommunications equipment, pharmaceuticals, and computers.

Such talks tend to require large and costly bureaucratic structures and often have undesirable third-country and domestic third-party side effects—as when Japan enlarges the U.S. import quota on beef and citrus at Australia's expense or the U.S. and Japanese governments settle a dispute over semiconductors by raising input costs to America's chip users. Still, bilateral product-specific talks are felt to have worked and are thus likely to be continued.

Unfair Competition by Foreign Exporters

Production subsidies, export subsidies, export credits, and dumping are among the trade practices that have provoked friction among trading partners. In the United States they often exemplify the "non-level playing field" of international trade. Multilateral efforts to create rules of conduct and guidelines for surveillance and control have not been wholly satisfactory. The Tokyo round of trade negotiations made progress toward the establishment of a subsidies code and of dumping guidelines and antidumping procedures, and an agreement worked out within the Organization for Economic Cooperation and Development (OECD) imposed limits on export credits. Although these efforts moved the system in the right direction, much remains to be done. The United States, for example, has accused Japanese producers of dumping semiconductors and the European Community of dumping subsidized wheat. In response to the former, the United States and Japan have established what amounts to a price-monitoring cartel that has been criticized by third countries; in response to the latter the United States now also dumps wheat.

The case of agriculture underscores the disruptive effects of production subsidies on world supply. As a result governments are forced to follow production subsidies with export subsidies and credits so as to move onto world markets the excess output they have stimulated. The European Community's Common Agricultural Policy (CAP) provides a classic example. By setting agricultural prices well above their market-clearing levels, the CAP has triggered supply responses that have converted the European Community from a food importer not many years ago to a net food exporter today. As domestic output exceeded domestic demand, official purchases at first soaked up excess output to maintain targeted prices, but growing stockpiles necessitated increasingly aggressive efforts to unload them on world markets, below cost if necessary. The flow of heavily subsidized produce from the European Community has been a destabilizing element on world markets and is a major source of trade friction.

Steel provides another example where heavily subsidized investment programs contributed to worldwide excess supply. The forced retrenchment that inevitably followed in Europe and Japan, as well as the United States, has been difficult and painful. The episode illustrates rather well the distortions that may be created by governments in the pursuit of industrial strategies.

How to Counter Unfair Foreign Export Practices

Export subsidies and credits raise capacity and depress price. A retaliatory policy that matches foreign subsidies and credits expands capacity further and depresses prices further. Unless the threat of retaliation forces the foreign country to reconsider, actual retaliation compounds the problem by misallocating domestic resources and burdening federal budgets.

When subsidized foreign products are sold in the U.S. market, a retaliatory import restriction may be considered. Its advantage is that it protects domestic producers from unfair foreign competition; its disadvantage is that it raises U.S. prices above world prices and thereby places U.S. users at a competitive disadvantage. If domestic producers need to be protected, outright income subsidies are superior economically but difficult politically.

Bilateral negotiations may be more promising, especially if they are coupled with a threat that failure to resolve the dispute will bring retaliation. But in the long run only concerted multilateral action combined with effective enforcement procedures is capable of solving the problem.

Cheap Foreign Labor

Some observers have argued that less-developed countries compete unfairly by paying low wages. The omnibus trade bill passed by the House of Representatives in 1986 raises this issue and suggests that unfair labor practices may be the cause of low wages abroad. As commonly expressed, however, the complaint is defective on several grounds. First, it fails to recognize the basic purpose of specialization, which is to exploit differences among countries in resource endowments as each specializes in products making intensive use of its abundant and hence relatively inexpensive factors of production. Labor, especially unskilled labor, tends to be the plentiful factor in developing countries, so that their competitive edge lies naturally in labor-intensive products.

Moreover, low wages per se are not evidence of unfair labor practices. Indeed, comparison of money wages contains no useful information about competitiveness whenever productivity differs. An American worker who is twice as productive as his foreign counterpart can receive twice the wage without losing competitiveness, because labor cost per unit of output will be identical at home and abroad. If American wages keep pace with productivity and foreigners' wages do likewise, competitiveness will remain unimpaired. If, however, American wages rise faster than productivity (as happened in several U.S. industries, including steel), unit labor costs will rise, and competitiveness will suffer.

Wages corrected for productivity are thus the proper units of comparison. Productivity gains result from the improvement of skill and from the accumulation of capital and human capital. American workers earn high incomes because they are skilled and because they work with relatively large quantities of capital and equally large quantities of skilled workers, such as scientists, engineers, and designers (so-called human capital).

As we have already seen, it is an abundance of capital and skills that enables advanced industrial nations to support advanced living standards and high wages. U.S. labor is generally better educated and more comprehensively trained, so that its direct (that is, embodied) productivity will tend to be higher than productivity abroad; but it is the presence of capital and human capital that enhances American labor's indirect (that is, disembodied) productivity.

Even when inexpensive labor is combined with modern technology, productivity considerations hold. Less-developed countries, with plentiful unskilled labor and scarce skilled labor, tend to conserve the latter and use the former. The resulting higher labor-capital ratios in production abroad generate lower labor productivity and hence lower wages.

The "cheap labor as unfair competition" argument thus does not have much to commend it. Lower wages in developing countries are generally consistent with lower productivity there. It is often wage growth in excess of productivity growth in advanced countries that precipitates losses in competitiveness. Since labor productivity is generally lower in developing countries, wages will be lower. There is nothing "unfair" about such competition, any more than the United States can be accused of competing unfairly by using its abundant natural resources.

Shortcomings of the Trading System

Dissatisfaction with GATT and with the multilateral trading system has been building steadily. GATT rules have little to say about agriculture, trade in services, or intellectual property rights, and the system's dispute settlement procedures leave much to be desired. Although several rounds of multilateral negotiations have brought substantial reductions in tariffs, other less transparent and often more costly barriers to trade have been erected, including quotas, orderly market arrangements (OMAs), voluntary export restraints (VERs) or voluntary restraint agreements (VRAs) more generally, and administrative guidelines and technical product standards that are difficult to measure and evaluate. Efforts to negotiate codes relating to subsidies and dumping have not yet been successfully concluded.

Multilateral Approaches

In the long run a strong and dynamic multilateral system of rules and codes of conduct and of effective sanctions and settlement procedures is needed to deal with many of today's trade problems. But the necessary reform requires the leadership of a hegemonic country or of a group of countries determined to bring it about. The United States, which once played that role, has become increasingly parochial in its interests but is still crucial to the success of any system. Europe, too, could play a leading role, but its perspective is even more parochial and short term, and its influence in GATT has been more to impede than to build. It may therefore be necessary for the United States to look for coalitions elsewhere, possibly with newly industrializing countries.

Recent U.S. trade policy, however, has followed two approaches. One has been to encourage multilateral procedures with energetic

U.S. participation in several GATT rounds and equally energetic efforts to place agricultural trade, trade in services, intellectual property rights, international investment, and dispute settlement on the agenda of the next round.

The other has been to bypass the multilateral framework in the pursuit of protection for weak and inefficient domestic industries, including textiles and apparel, steel, automobiles, machine tools, sugar, and dairy products, and to do so with quotas, orderly marketing arrangements, and voluntary export restraint programs and, in the case of textiles, by means of the Multi-Fibre Arrangement (MFA). A recent agreement on semiconductors, also concluded outside the multilateral framework, allocates responsibility for world prices to the United States and Japan.

What is striking about this pattern is that the multilateral approach is reserved for U.S. industries with comparative advantage, whose interests would be furthered by nondiscrimination in world trade. Where U.S. producers have comparative disadvantage, nondiscriminatory multilateral arrangements have been eschewed in favor of individually and independently negotiated restrictive measures.

Note

1. If the United States has market power in the commodities subject to restrictions, their world market price will fall while their prices in the United States rise, implying that foreign competitors will see their costs fall.

5
The Policy Agenda

Recent developments in U.S. trade and competitiveness are a result of three major forces. First, macroeconomic events and macroeconomic policies in the United States have been a principal force behind the deterioration of the U.S. trade balance, the erosion of competitiveness, and the emergence of the country as a debtor nation. Second in importance are gradual but far-reaching changes in the global competitive environment. Third are unfair practices.

Although unfair trade practices have received considerable attention from politicians, they are probably the least important of the three factors. They cannot help much to explain the deterioration in the U.S. trade position in the 1980s, because they have not changed much. Moreover, even the most optimistic estimates suggest that greater fairness in world commerce would leave much of our trade problem intact.

Macroeconomic Policies

It is safe to suppose that a significant improvement in the current account deficit, let alone a return to surplus, cannot take place without a significant improvement in the federal budget situation. The public sector, having been a primary cause of trade and exchange rate developments in recent years, must play a decisive role in any turnaround because there is little hope for a significant rise in the private savings ratio and because the economy cannot afford a massive retrenchment in private capital formation.

Senior U.S. government officials believe that significant improvement in the U.S. trade balance could be achieved by means of macroeconomic stimulation in Germany and Japan. An expansion of aggregate demand there would certainly raise imports from the United States but would leave the greater part of the U.S. trade deficit intact without significant improvements in domestic macroeconomic policies. Rather than mere expansion abroad, foreign expansion coupled with realignment of domestic policies is needed.

The Changing World Economy

Irreversible changes are taking place in global competition. They are most pronounced in standardized labor-intensive manufactures and in certain capital-intensive products of heavy industry where the newly industrializing countries are carving out strong cost advantages. These changes affect industries that have been major sources of employment in advanced countries and so create political difficulties.

The policy options for dealing with these changes are limited. If productivity cannot be raised and product quality cannot be improved, competitiveness is unlikely to be regained. The evidence indicates that in such cases the cost per job "saved" through trade intervention tends to be several times higher than the wages of incumbent workers. Moreover, trade intervention tends to raise wages and input costs beyond the industry being protected and thereby spreads the damage to other parts of the economy. Where competitiveness cannot be regained, the long-run solution is adjustment and relocation.

Unfair Trade

Americans feel that foreigners are taking unfair advantage of world trade. This is a major issue, requiring the urgent attention of policy makers, because no system based on law and rules can long survive when they are violated. The agenda for the next GATT round has many items whose resolution would improve the system, but even so most of America's trade problems would remain unchanged. The limited contribution that greater fairness can make to resolution of our trade problems must be kept in mind, so that the public can make a proper assessment of the required domestic remedies.

Policy Strategies

Although recent developments in trade and competitiveness are the joint result of macroeconomic influences and of short- and long-run structural factors, policy makers may attempt to deal with each element separately and independently of the others. This is more or less the approach taken by the U.S. government, but it does not rule out a more coordinated approach that would endeavor to improve the general policy environment while attacking the structural problems. This approach opens up options not available under the decentralized, uncoordinated approach. Before evaluating the coordination option, however, we examine the major relevant policy instruments.

Budgetary Policies. Since the federal budget deficit has been widely identified as a major cause of America's current account difficulties, their solution lies necessarily with budgetary policy. Among several approaches to deficit reduction, the one on which the debate has focused consists of tax increases or expenditure reductions. This approach has proved highly intractable in light of conflicting priorities between the White House and the Congress.

A variant of this approach that would work more slowly but would affect expectations immediately would fix the relative real growth rates of expenditures and revenues and thereby let relative real revenue growth reduce the deficit over time. The focus of the debate needs to shift from its present preoccupation with measuring burdens by taxes or tax rates toward a more comprehensive measure of the burden of carrying the public sector that includes, for example, real interest rates. The president would then have to come to terms with the fact that taxes and tax rates are a partial measure at best of what it costs the average worker or citizen to maintain public programs. The policy dispute between the president and the Congress has also become stuck on an excessively short-run view of the burden that lures the public into ignoring the intertemporal aspects of the burden. The Washington stalemate is a peculiar policy artifact, produced by excessively narrow definitions of the "cost" of government.

The problem is also, however, one of trade-offs and of burden distribution. The burden of the deficit of the 1980s has fallen disproportionately on tradables producers. Interest rates have played a part, but only a part, in the adjustment process, the weight of the realignment having fallen on real exchange rates. Exchange-rate-sensitive tradables sectors have been hurt while interest-rate-sensitive non-tradables sectors have been less burdened. Agriculture has been especially hard hit, given its sensitivity to both interest rates and exchange rates.

A reduction in the budget deficit by means of tax increases would shift the burden from sectors sensitive to exchange rates and interest rates to the general taxpayer. If the rest of the world could be persuaded to increase its absorption of goods and thus reduce its willingness to lend to the United States and if this global tightening of supply did not directly reduce the budget deficit by much, interest rates in the United States and in the rest of the world would have to rise sharply. If the problem is "solved" by means of inflationary finance, wealth owners and creditors generally will bear the weight of the necessary adjustment. Hence no single solution will be universally approved, but a package that distributes the burden may be. The Reagan administration, however, has painted itself into a corner, limiting its policy options by insisting that budgetary policies have no effect on real interest rates.

It is important to recall that the economy-wide imbalance is not merely one between total domestic output and absorption, that is, between total public and private saving and investment. The extraordinary real appreciation of the dollar was necessitated by the large weight of nontradables (including commercial and residential construction) in the demand expansion of the 1980s. If foreign capital and foreign resources had been less abundantly available, the greater pressure on interest rates would have crowded out some nontradables expenditures. If more nontradables had been available for use by the public sector, a smaller increase in the real value of the dollar would have been needed to cover the remaining difference. Hence a tax increase is not merely a means of financing federal expenditures but a way of reducing the sectoral nonneutrality of recent growth in domestic demand.

The concern has recently been expressed by some observers and government officials that budgetary contraction at this time could risk a recession. This is a legitimate worry and one that many critics anticipated when they pressed for corrective action during more favorable cyclical conditions. At this stage in the present cycle, with the world economy relatively soft, coordinated actions combining U.S. fiscal correction, foreign macroeconomic stimulation, and new growth-oriented solutions of the global debt crisis may be especially promising. We take up this issue now.

Trade Policy. Trade policy is attracting a growing following, at least in the Congress. It is attractive because it promises so much to so many. To some it is a way of reducing the trade deficit without having to wait for better budgetary policies. For others it provides revenue suitable for budget balancing or financing trade adjustment assistance. Still others see it as retaliation designed to punish trading partners for unfair practices. Everybody sees something in trade policy, but most will be disappointed. Trade policy is being dangerously oversold in the nation's capital; its results, as in the past, are likely to be damaging to the nation's larger interests.

Indeed, it is quite safe to predict, with only the slightest risk of being wrong, that trade policy is unlikely to improve the trade balance significantly unless domestic policies are changed; and if they are, trade policy is not needed for this purpose. What is certain, however, is that trade policy will impair U.S. export competitiveness.

Rather than improve economic efficiency and performance in protected industries, it will merely sustain inefficient firms at substantial expense to the public. The evidence overwhelmingly contradicts the claim that trade policy is an effective means of improving an industry's competitiveness. Its typical effect is exactly the opposite: it takes away competitive pressures.

It is unlikely to save many jobs. Substantial evidence suggests that productivity growth and competition from substitute products, not import competition, have been the major reasons for job losses. Indeed, there is always a trade-off between maintaining competitiveness—predominantly by improvements in productivity, which tend to reduce the number of workers needed to produce a given output level—and preserving existing jobs.

Protection is quite likely, however, to provoke retaliation from at least some trading partners, especially the larger ones. To the extent that it is illegal under the General Agreement on Tariffs and Trade (GATT), affected parties will be entitled to compensation.

Nor is trade policy as retaliation against unfair foreign trade practices any more promising unless it is used as a threat. If retaliatory action is actually taken, it may invite counteraction, as in the dispute between the United States and Canada over lumber. Even when the foreign country does not take counteraction but does not change its practices, trade policy will have compounded the economic damage at home.

One of the great weaknesses of trade policy is its relative inefficiency. It distorts domestic price signals and thus encourages inefficient resource allocations, precisely of the kind the Congress tried so hard to eliminate with the Tax Reform Act of 1986. Trade policy can be counterproductive, especially when it is practiced on a broad and general scale as contemplated in H.R. 4800, the House bill of 1986. An industry's nominal protection is no guarantee of real protection, because the rest of the intervention structure can easily cancel some or all of the benefit. Restrictions on imported inputs can easily leave less rather than more value added to be shared among the factors of production in an industry. An astonishing feature of H.R. 4800 is that it passed without anyone's knowing the implied effective rates of protection.

Strategic trade policy also has little to offer policy makers. In theory it brings gains in the terms of trade, as well as gains from exploitation of economies of scale, under relatively precise and restrictive assumptions about the structure of an industry, the constancy of government policy, and the absence of foreign retaliation. And even in theory it is surgical and selective, requires choices among winners and losers, and does not lend itself to administration by broad guidelines and bureaucratic standards.

In short, for the major problems facing the United States in international trade—macroeconomic imbalances, deep-seated changes in competitiveness, and unfair trade practices abroad—trade policy with its traditional instrumentalities of tariffs and quantitative interventions is simply not suitable. It cannot offset the effects of poor macroeconomic policies; it will not improve the quality of American products or the quantity of research or halt America's decline in abundance of capital and skill; and if used to retaliate against unfair foreign practices, it will hurt more than help. Macroeconomic policies are needed to deal with the first problems, domestic infrastructure policies with the second, and negotiations with the third.

Trade Negotiations

This rather negative assessment of trade policy and its standard instrumentalities does not extend to trade negotiations, which offer significant opportunities not only in the struggle against unfair foreign trade practices but for bringing health, order, and discipline to the global trading system. But the form, structure, and country and commodity coverage of negotiations make a difference.

Limited Negotiations. Negotiations limited by country or commodity coverage have been used extensively by the United States for offensive as well as defensive purposes. As an offensive weapon in the fight against unfair trade practices, bilateral trade talks with Japan and other countries have played a major role and will no doubt be continued. They are far from ideal, however, because they tend to be costly in labor and time and because their specificity as to countries and commodities often creates nontrivial third-party and third-country effects. A world partitioned by a multitude of exclusive trading arrangements is bound to be inefficient and subject to many zero-sum-game situations.

Restricted negotiations used defensively by the United States have led to trade policy that has been viewed from abroad as unfair and from the inside as costly. The Multi-Fibre Arrangement in textiles is an example, as are bilateral pacts and voluntary export restraint agreements in products such as steel, textiles and apparel, machine tools, and sugar. In these cases involving U.S. producers with declining comparative advantage, the approach has been to eschew multilateral treatment and to conduct trade policy at the executive rather than the legislative level. This approach thus violates the unconditional most-favored-nation principle and denies the public the full benefit of legislative debate and decision.

Multilateral Negotiations. The multilateral trading system is in need of overhaul, and the success of the coming Uruguay round of global talks will surely be measured by its achievements in this area. This is by far the most difficult round, because the issues are more complex and the players more numerous. It is also more difficult for the United States, whose hegemony in the world economy has been declining and whose internal consensus on free and open trade has been eroded by the sharp rise in foreign competition.

Americans think they know what they want from this round in areas such as services, agriculture, intellectual property rights, investment, subsidies, and dispute settlement. And their negotiators are preparing to argue for these things on broad principles, even though we, like others, have violated those principles. In the end, however, the outcome will depend heavily on reciprocal concessions, and there is no consensus yet on U.S. concessions.

Trade liberalization in agriculture, for example, could bring significant benefits and would be less disruptive to any one country if it occurred in a coordinated fashion. But trade liberalization in this area cannot proceed very far without changes in domestic agricultural support programs, not so much in their basic objectives of preserving the family farm, maintaining green space, and so on as in the means employed. To bring about changes in domestic support programs will take all the political leadership the White House and Congress can muster.

Services trade is another problem requiring more than adroit negotiation with other countries. The basic forces determining comparative advantage work here much as they work in goods. America's competitive strength lies in capital- and skill-intensive services (like telecommunications), its comparative disadvantage in labor-intensive services (like construction and data entry). Hence imports in services containing relatively low skills are bound to grow and to generate the kinds of protectionist pressures that have been felt by producers of standardized labor-intensive goods.

Conclusion

Among the factors that have contributed to America's trade problems, macroeconomic policies in general and budgetary policies in particular rank first in importance. In comparison, unfair foreign trade practices have played a much smaller role, but they are receiving much of the attention and blame in the contemporary policy debate.

Unfair trade practices unquestionably present a major problem for the world community, as does the creaky and antiquated institutional structure of the trading system. But even on a more level playing field Americans would carry a serious competitive handicap in the absence of fundamental improvements in macroeconomic policy.

Beyond these issues the United States faces long-run challenges in a rapidly changing global trading environment. The competitive position of U.S. producers is endangered whenever the quality of capital and labor is allowed to decline in relation to that of other countries. When American capital and labor are no more productive than their foreign competitors, they cannot long sustain their higher prices. Long-run competitiveness is not secured by import surcharges and other currently popular trade measures, and without competitiveness U.S. living standards cannot be protected. Public policy, as well as management and labor attitudes and practices, has become increasingly incompatible with global competitive realities and must be more firmly focused on recapturing and preserving America's international competitive position. The possibilities and prospects are plentiful, in industry as well as in high-value-added services, and those who see the nation as a producer of low-value-added services are wrong in their interpretation of recent experience and of future prospects.

Appendix A
The U.S. Economy in the 1980s

TABLE A–1
U.S. Trade Balance, Selected Industries, 1980–1985
(billions of dollars)

Industry	1980	1981	1982	1983	1984	1985	1980–1985
Agriculture	19.6	21.2	16.5	15.2	15.3	7.3	−12.3
Mining	−62.4	−60.9	−45.1	−37.4	−37.1	−32.6	29.8
Manufacturing	20.7	12.9	−2.0	−34.8	−84.3	−104.3	−125.0
Food and kindred products	1.7	2.2	1.5	0.7	−0.9	−2.5	−4.2
Tobacco manufactures	1.0	1.1	1.1	0.8	1.1	1.2	0.2
Textile mill products	0.5	−0.2	−0.5	−1.0	−1.9	−2.2	−2.7
Apparel products	−4.9	−6.1	−7.2	−8.9	−12.9	−14.7	−9.8
Lumber and wood products	0.1	−0.6	−0.2	−1.6	−2.1	−2.4	−2.5
Furniture and fixtures	−0.6	−0.6	−0.8	−1.3	−1.9	−2.7	−2.1
Paper and allied products	−0.8	−1.0	−1.3	−1.7	−3.1	−3.6	−2.8

Printing and publishing	0.6	0.8	0.8	0.7	0.3	0.1	0.5
Chemical products	14.1	13.8	12.4	10.4	10.3	9.0	−5.1
Petroleum and coal products	−10.6	−11.8	−9.3	−12.1	−16.1	−12.9	−2.3
Rubber and plastic products	−0.1	−0.1	−0.3	−0.7	−1.4	−2.0	−1.9
Leather products	−2.9	−3.4	−4.0	−4.8	−6.3	−7.2	−4.3
Stone, clay, and glass	−0.3	−0.4	−0.5	−1.1	−1.9	−2.5	−2.2
Primary metal products	−6.9	−12.4	−10.5	−11.0	−16.8	−15.7	−8.8
Fabricated metal products	2.5	2.9	2.5	1.4	−0.3	−2.0	−4.5
Machinery, except electrical	24.9	27.8	23.9	15.8	9.6	6.2	−18.7
Electrical equipment	0.9	−0.4	−1.9	−6.4	−15.2	−19.0	−19.9
Transportation equipment	−1.5	−0.9	−7.0	−11.7	−22.1	−27.9	−26.4
Instruments	3.0	2.8	3.0	2.3	1.0	−0.2	−3.2
Miscellaneous	−2.5	−3.7	−4.4	−4.5	−7.8	−9.4	−6.9

SOURCES: Department of Commerce, Bureau of the Census, Foreign Trade Division, Report EA675, *U.S. Exports*, and Report IA275, *U.S. Imports for Consumption and General Imports*, various issues.

TABLE A-2

U.S. IMPORTS, SELECTED INDUSTRIES, 1980–1985

(billions of dollars)

Industry	1980	1981	1982	1983	1984	1985	1980–1985 (percent)
Agriculture	10.5	10.2	10.0	10.7	12.3	12.8	21.5
Mining	70.7	70.0	53.7	43.6	43.5	39.0	−44.8
Manufacturing	150.6	171.4	170.4	194.4	257.6	280.1	85.9
Food and kindred products	10.4	10.7	9.6	10.3	12.0	12.5	20.6
Tobacco manufactures	0.1	0.2	0.2	0.4	0.1	0.1	−16.1
Textile mill products	2.0	2.5	2.2	2.6	3.5	3.6	77.7
Apparel products	6.5	7.8	8.4	9.9	13.9	15.7	140.1
Lumber and wood products	3.7	3.6	3.1	4.4	4.8	5.1	39.9
Furniture and fixtures	1.1	1.2	1.3	1.8	2.5	3.2	197.7
Paper and allied products	5.4	5.8	5.4	5.8	7.4	7.5	37.8

Industry							
Printing and publishing	0.5	0.5	0.6	0.7	1.1	1.2	134.7
Chemical products	7.0	7.9	7.6	9.3	12.0	12.8	82.9
Petroleum and coal products	13.4	15.8	15.7	17.4	21.2	18.3	36.2
Rubber and plastic products	2.7	3.1	2.9	3.4	4.4	4.7	72.1
Leather products	3.4	3.9	4.5	5.3	6.8	7.7	128.6
Stone, clay, and glass	2.3	2.5	2.4	2.9	3.8	4.3	89.9
Primary metal products	15.6	18.7	15.4	15.1	22.1	20.4	30.8
Fabricated metal products	4.4	5.1	5.2	5.3	6.8	7.8	75.8
Machinery, except electrical	13.2	15.1	15.0	17.4	27.6	31.3	137.0
Electrical equipment	15.5	18.8	20.1	24.5	35.3	38.0	144.4
Transportation equipment	30.7	34.1	36.7	42.5	54.3	65.9	114.7
Instruments	4.7	5.6	5.4	6.0	7.7	8.8	87.6
Miscellaneous	4.4	5.4	5.9	6.1	9.7	11.1	155.5

SOURCE: Department of Commerce, Bureau of the Census, Foreign Trade Division, Report IA275, *U.S. Imports for Consumption and General Imports*, various issues.

TABLE A–3

U.S. EXPORTS, SELECTED INDUSTRIES, 1980–1985

(billions of dollars)

Industry	1980	1981	1982	1983	1984	1985	1980–1985 (percent)
Agriculture	30.1	31.5	26.5	26.0	27.6	20.1	−33.3
Mining	8.3	9.1	8.6	6.2	6.4	6.4	−23.3
Manufacturing	171.4	184.2	168.4	159.6	173.3	175.8	2.6
Food and kindred products	12.1	12.9	11.1	11.0	11.1	10.1	−17.1
Tobacco manufactures	1.1	1.3	1.3	1.2	1.2	1.3	17.2
Textile mill products	2.5	2.3	1.8	1.6	1.5	1.5	−41.3
Apparel products	1.6	1.6	1.2	1.1	1.1	1.0	−36.5
Lumber and wood products	3.7	3.1	2.9	2.9	2.7	2.7	−27.8
Furniture and fixtures	0.5	0.6	0.6	0.5	0.6	0.5	7.1
Paper and allied products	4.7	4.8	4.2	4.1	4.3	3.9	−16.8

Printing and publishing	1.1	1.3	1.4	1.3	1.4	1.3	12.0
Chemical products	21.1	21.7	20.0	19.7	22.3	21.8	3.3
Petroleum and coal products	2.9	4.0	6.4	5.3	5.1	5.4	90.7
Rubber and plastic products	2.7	3.0	2.6	2.6	2.9	2.8	3.4
Leather products	0.5	0.5	0.5	0.5	0.5	0.5	−6.3
Stone, clay, and glass	1.9	2.1	1.9	1.8	1.9	1.8	−6.8
Primary metal products	8.7	6.3	4.9	4.1	5.4	4.7	−45.5
Fabricated metal products	6.9	7.9	7.7	6.7	6.5	5.8	−16.8
Machinery, except electrical	38.1	42.9	38.9	33.2	37.3	37.5	−1.6
Electrical equipment	16.4	18.4	18.2	18.0	20.2	18.9	15.4
Transportation equipment	29.2	33.2	29.7	30.9	32.2	38.0	30.2
Instruments	7.7	8.4	8.4	8.3	8.7	8.6	12.1
Miscellaneous	1.9	1.8	1.4	1.5	1.9	1.8	−6.9

Source: Department of Commerce, Bureau of the Census, Foreign Trade Division, Report EA675, *U.S. Exports*, various issues.

TABLE A-4
Structure of U.S. Imports, 1980–1985

Industry	1980	1981	1982	1983	1984	1985
Percentage of total U.S. imports						
Agriculture	4.4	3.9	4.1	4.2	3.8	3.7
Mining	29.5	27.0	22.2	17.0	13.5	11.4
Manufacturing	62.9	66.1	70.3	75.7	79.8	81.5
Percentage of U.S. manufacturing imports						
Food and kindred products	6.9	6.2	5.6	5.3	4.7	4.5
Tobacco manufactures	0.1	0.1	0.1	0.2	—	—
Textile mill products	1.4	1.4	1.3	1.3	1.3	1.3
Apparel products	4.3	4.5	4.9	5.1	5.4	5.6
Lumber and wood products	2.4	2.1	1.8	2.3	1.9	1.8
Furniture and fixtures	0.7	0.7	0.8	0.9	1.0	1.1
Paper and allied products	3.6	3.4	3.2	3.0	2.9	2.7

Printing and publishing	0.3	0.3	0.3	0.3	0.4	0.4
Chemical products	4.6	4.6	4.5	4.8	4.7	4.6
Petroleum and coal products	8.9	9.2	9.2	8.9	8.2	6.5
Rubber and plastic products	1.8	1.8	1.7	1.8	1.7	1.7
Leather products	2.2	2.3	2.6	2.7	2.6	2.8
Stone, clay, and glass	1.5	1.4	1.4	1.5	1.5	1.5
Primary metal products	10.4	10.9	9.0	7.8	8.6	7.3
Fabricated metal products	2.9	2.9	3.0	2.7	2.6	2.8
Machinery, except electrical	8.8	8.8	8.8	8.9	10.7	11.2
Electrical equipment	10.3	11.0	11.8	12.6	13.7	13.5
Transportation equipment	20.4	19.9	21.5	21.9	21.1	23.5
Instruments	3.1	3.3	3.2	3.1	3.0	3.1
Miscellaneous	2.9	3.2	3.4	3.1	3.8	4.0

SOURCE: Department of Commerce, Bureau of the Census, Foreign Trade Division, Report IA275, *U.S. Imports for Consumption and General Imports*, various issues.

TABLE A-5
STRUCTURE OF U.S. EXPORTS, 1980–1985

Industry	1980	1981	1982	1983	1984	1985
Percentage of total U.S. exports						
Agriculture	13.9	13.7	12.8	13.3	13.0	9.7
Mining	3.8	4.0	4.2	3.2	3.0	3.1
Manufacturing	79.1	80.5	81.3	81.4	81.7	84.9
Percentage of U.S. manufacturing exports						
Food and kindred products	7.1	7.0	6.6	6.9	6.4	5.7
Tobacco manufactures	0.6	0.7	0.8	0.7	0.7	0.7
Textile mill products	1.5	1.3	1.0	1.0	0.9	0.8
Apparel products	0.9	0.9	0.7	0.7	0.6	0.6
Lumber and wood products	2.2	1.7	1.7	1.8	1.6	1.5
Furniture and fixtures	0.3	0.3	0.3	0.3	0.3	0.3
Paper and allied products	2.7	2.6	2.5	2.6	2.5	2.2

Printing and publishing	0.7	0.7	0.8	0.8	0.8	0.7
Chemical products	12.3	11.8	11.9	12.3	12.8	12.4
Petroleum and coal products	1.7	2.2	3.8	3.3	3.0	3.1
Rubber and plastic products	1.6	1.6	1.6	1.7	1.7	1.6
Leather products	0.3	0.3	0.3	0.3	0.3	0.3
Stone, clay, and glass	1.1	1.1	1.1	1.1	1.1	1.0
Primary metal products	5.1	3.4	2.9	2.5	3.1	2.7
Fabricated metal products	4.0	4.3	4.6	4.2	3.8	3.3
Machinery, except electrical	22.2	23.3	23.1	20.8	21.5	21.3
Electrical equipment	9.6	10.0	10.8	11.3	11.6	10.8
Transportation equipment	17.0	18.0	17.6	19.3	18.6	21.6
Instruments	4.5	4.6	5.0	5.2	5.0	4.9
Miscellaneous	1.1	1.0	0.9	0.9	1.1	1.0

SOURCE: Department of Commerce, Bureau of the Census, Foreign Trade Division, Report EA675, *U.S. Exports*, various issues.

TABLE A-6
U.S. EXPORTS AS RELATED TO OUTPUT, 1980–1985
(percentage of GDP)

Industry	1980	1981	1982	1983	1984	1985	1980–1985 (percent)
Total	8.1	7.6	6.7	5.8	5.7	5.2	-35.2
Agriculture	38.9	34.2	29.6	35.0	29.3	21.9	-43.6
Manufacturing	29.5	28.6	26.5	23.4	22.6	22.1	-25.1
Food and kindred products	23.2	22.3	18.0	17.3	16.3	14.3	-38.3
Tobacco manufactures	14.8	15.9	14.5	9.8	9.6	10.2	-31.0
Textile mill products	16.7	14.6	11.9	9.2	8.9	8.9	-47.0
Apparel products	9.4	8.8	6.5	5.2	5.0	5.0	-47.0
Lumber and wood products	19.8	17.8	17.9	13.9	11.4	11.7	-40.8
Furniture and fixtures	5.2	6.6	5.9	4.9	4.3	3.7	-30.2
Paper and allied products	20.3	18.9	15.8	14.8	13.5	11.2	-44.7

Printing and publishing	3.5	3.7	3.5	3.1	2.9	2.4	−31.8
Chemical products	46.4	40.6	36.2	33.0	34.6	33.1	−28.7
Petroleum and coal products	17.0	20.2	26.2	18.8	17.3	17.0	0.4
Rubber and plastic products	15.9	15.4	13.6	12.0	11.9	10.8	−31.9
Leather products	13.1	12.1	12.1	12.0	15.0	14.5	10.7
Stone, clay, and glass	10.1	11.1	10.2	8.8	8.1	7.3	−27.4
Primary metal products	19.6	12.8	13.8	13.4	15.0	13.7	−30.4
Fabricated metal products	15.1	16.0	16.6	14.1	12.2	10.5	−30.3
Machinery, except electrical	49.5	49.8	48.6	44.1	41.9	39.6	−20.1
Electrical equipment	29.8	30.3	29.4	26.6	26.5	23.4	−21.4
Transportation equipment	53.2	55.2	48.1	39.0	33.6	38.1	−28.5
Instruments	40.5	37.8	37.0	34.6	34.9	33.6	−17.0
Miscellaneous	19.8	15.0	12.9	14.6	15.9	15.0	−24.3

SOURCES: U.S. Department of Commerce, Bureau of the Census, Foreign Trade Division, Report EA275, *U.S. Exports*; and U.S. Department of Commerce, Bureau of Economic Analysis, *National Income and Product Accounts*.

TABLE A-7
U.S. Imports as Related to Output, 1980–1985
(percentage of GDP)

Industry	1980	1981	1982	1983	1984	1985	1980–1985 (percent)
Total	8.9	8.6	7.8	7.7	8.7	8.7	−2.7
Agriculture	13.6	11.1	11.2	14.1	12.9	14.0	2.7
Manufacturing	25.9	26.6	26.9	28.5	33.6	35.2	35.7
Food and kindred products	19.9	18.5	15.6	16.0	17.7	17.8	−10.3
Tobacco manufactures	1.3	2.5	2.5	3.4	0.7	0.6	−50.4
Textile mill products	13.7	15.6	15.0	15.1	20.1	21.9	60.5
Apparel products	38.3	41.7	44.6	48.8	65.3	76.6	100.3
Lumber and wood products	19.5	21.3	19.1	21.6	20.5	22.4	14.8
Furniture and fixtures	12.6	13.4	14.3	16.9	19.2	24.4	93.7
Paper and allied products	23.6	23.0	20.5	20.9	23.1	21.7	−8.4

Printing and publishing	1.6	1.5	1.4	1.5	2.3	2.3	42.9
Chemical products	15.4	14.7	13.7	15.7	18.7	19.4	26.3
Petroleum and coal products	79.9	79.9	64.2	61.5	71.6	57.3	−28.3
Rubber and plastic products	16.3	16.1	15.2	15.5	17.7	18.5	13.4
Leather products	86.6	90.1	109.7	139.4	193.9	234.0	170.1
Stone, clay, and glass	11.9	13.1	13.2	14.2	16.2	17.6	47.9
Primary metal products	35.3	37.6	43.5	49.8	62.0	58.9	67.0
Fabricated metal products	9.6	10.2	11.2	11.2	12.7	14.1	47.3
Machinery, except electrical	17.2	17.5	18.7	23.1	31.1	33.1	92.4
Electrical equipment	28.2	31.0	32.5	36.1	46.4	47.0	66.4
Transportation equipment	55.9	56.7	59.4	53.7	56.7	66.0	18.0
Instruments	24.7	25.3	23.8	25.2	31.0	34.3	38.7
Miscellaneous	45.4	46.3	52.7	58.7	81.6	94.3	107.8

SOURCES: U.S. Department of Commerce, Bureau of the Census, Foreign Trade Division, Report IA275, *U.S. Imports for Consumption and General Imports;* and U.S. Department of Commerce, Bureau of Economic Analysis, *National Income and Product Accounts.*

TABLE A–8

U.S. Imports as Related to Apparent Consumption, 1980–1985

(percentage of apparent consumption)

Industry	1980	1981	1982	1983	1984	1985	1980–1985 (percent)
Total	8.8	8.6	7.7	7.5	8.4	8.4	−5.2
Agriculture	18.2	14.4	13.7	18.2	15.6	15.2	−16.7
Manufacturing	26.9	27.2	26.8	27.1	30.3	31.1	15.7
Food and kindred products	20.6	19.2	16.0	16.1	17.5	17.2	−16.2
Tobacco manufactures	1.5	2.9	2.9	3.6	0.8	0.7	−52.6
Textile mill products	14.1	15.5	14.6	14.3	18.0	19.4	37.6
Apparel products	29.7	31.3	32.3	34.0	40.7	44.6	50.4
Lumber and wood products	19.6	20.6	18.9	20.1	18.8	20.2	3.4
Furniture and fixtures	11.7	12.5	13.2	15.1	16.7	20.2	72.2
Paper and allied products	22.9	22.1	19.6	19.7	21.1	19.6	−14.3

Printing and publishing	1.6	1.5	1.5	1.6	2.3	2.3	40.3
Chemical products	22.3	19.9	17.7	19.0	22.2	22.5	1.0
Petroleum and coal products	49.0	50.0	46.6	43.1	46.4	40.9	-16.7
Rubber and plastic products	16.3	16.0	15.0	15.0	16.7	17.2	5.7
Leather products	49.9	50.6	55.5	61.3	69.5	73.2	46.7
Stone, clay, and glass	11.7	12.8	12.8	13.4	15.0	16.0	36.5
Primary metal products	30.5	30.1	33.5	36.5	42.2	40.6	33.0
Fabricated metal products	10.1	10.8	11.8	11.5	12.6	13.6	34.3
Machinery, except electrical	25.4	25.9	26.7	29.2	34.9	35.4	39.3
Electrical equipment	28.7	30.8	31.5	33.0	38.7	38.0	32.6
Transportation equipment	54.4	55.9	53.4	46.8	46.1	51.6	-5.2
Instruments	29.3	28.9	27.4	27.8	32.3	28.5	-2.8
Miscellaneous	36.1	35.2	37.7	40.8	49.3	52.6	45.5

NOTE: Apparent consumption is defined as domestic output less exports plus imports.
SOURCES: U.S. Department of Commerce, Bureau of the Census, Foreign Trade Division, Report IA275, *U.S. Imports for Consumption and General Imports*; and U.S. Department of Commerce, Bureau of Economic Analysis, *National Income and Product Accounts*.

TABLE A–9
U.S. MERCHANDISE TRADE BALANCE WITH SELECTED COUNTRIES AND REGIONS, 1980–1985
(billions of dollars)

Country/Region	1980	1981	1982	1983	1984	1985
World	−36.2	−39.6	−42.6	−69.4	−123.3	−148.5
Industrial countries	−0.1	−13.5	−26.5	−36.5	−73.6	−98.1
Japan	−12.2	−18.1	−19.0	−21.7	−36.8	−49.5
Canada	−6.6	−7.3	−13.1	−14.3	−20.4	−22.2
European Community	16.3	8.7	3.5	−1.6	−13.3	−22.5
United Kingdon	2.4	−0.9	−2.9	−2.3	−2.8	−4.3
Germany	−1.3	−1.6	−3.2	−4.5	−8.7	−12.2
Developing countries	−35.2	−25.6	−14.1	−27.2	−41.7	−39.7
Oil-exporting countries	−40.2	−29.9	−9.1	−8.2	−11.9	−9.6
Non-oil-exporting countries	4.9	4.3	−5.0	−19.0	−29.8	−30.1
Africa	−19.8	−14.3	−10.5	−9.3	−8.9	−7.7
Asia	−2.5	−6.8	−4.8	−10.5	−18.1	−19.5
Western Hemisphere	−0.2	1.3	−6.0	−17.9	−20.4	−18.1
Brazil	0.4	−1.2	−1.2	−2.8	−5.6	−5.0
Mexico	2.3	3.8	−4.0	−7.9	−6.3	−5.8
NICs	−1.6	−4.5	−13.7	−23.4	−33.3	−34.4

NOTE: The figures for the European Community include only data for countries that were members before 1985. The newly industrializing countries (NICs) include Brazil, Hong Kong, Mexico, Singapore, South Korea, and Taiwan.
SOURCES: International Monetary Fund, *Direction of Trade Statistics*; and U.S. Department of Commerce, Bureau of the Census, *Highlights of U.S. Export and Import Trade*, FT990.

TABLE A–10

REGIONAL DISTRIBUTION OF U.S. EXPORTS, 1970–1985

(percent)

Country/Region	1970	1980	1981	1982	1983	1984	1985
Total exports (billions of dollars)	43	221	234	212	201	218	213
Industrial countries	66.0	56.8	55.5	55.2	58.7	59.9	60.8
Japan	10.7	9.4	9.3	9.9	10.9	10.8	10.6
Canada	21.0	16.0	16.9	15.9	19.1	21.3	22.2
European Community	26.6	24.7	22.4	22.6	22.1	21.6	21.5
United Kingdom	5.9	5.8	5.3	5.0	5.3	5.6	5.3
Germany	6.3	4.7	4.4	4.4	4.4	4.2	4.2
Developing countries	32.2	39.4	40.6	40.9	37.6	35.9	35.4
Africa	2.7	2.2	2.4	2.2	2.1	2.2	2.2
Asia	7.6	9.9	9.3	10.3	11.9	11.0	11.2
Western Hemisphere	13.4	15.5	15.7	13.4	11.4	12.1	14.6
Brazil	2.0	2.0	1.6	1.6	1.3	1.2	1.5
Mexico	3.9	6.9	7.6	5.6	4.5	5.5	6.4
NICs	9.7	15.4	15.6	14.4	14.2	14.8	16.4

NOTE: The figures for the European Community include only data for countries that were members before 1985. The newly industrializing countries (NICs) include Brazil, Hong Kong, Mexico, Singapore, South Korea, and Taiwan.
SOURCES: International Monetary Fund, *Direction of Trade Statistics*; and U.S. Department of Commerce, Bureau of the Census, *Highlights of U.S. Export and Import Trade*, FT990.

TABLE A–11
REGIONAL DISTRIBUTION OF U.S. IMPORTS, 1970–1985
(percent)

Country/Region	1970	1980	1981	1982	1983	1984	1985
Total imports (billions of dollars)	42	257	273	255	270	341	361
Industrial countries	71.4	49.2	52.4	56.4	57.2	59.8	63.0
Japan	14.7	12.8	14.6	15.7	16.1	17.7	20.0
Canada	27.8	16.3	17.1	18.4	19.5	19.6	19.2
European Community	23.2	14.9	16.0	17.4	17.0	17.7	18.9
United Kingdom	5.5	4.0	4.4	4.9	4.8	4.4	4.3
Germany	7.8	4.8	4.9	5.3	4.9	5.2	5.9
Developing countries	26.6	47.5	44.1	39.6	38.0	35.1	31.9
Africa	2.4	3.1	2.7	2.9	2.7	2.5	3.4
Asia	6.7	7.9	8.6	9.5	10.6	10.9	12.0
Western Hemisphere	11.9	13.0	12.8	13.6	14.2	12.7	13.6
Brazil	1.7	1.6	1.8	1.8	2.0	2.4	2.3
Mexico	3.1	5.0	5.1	6.2	6.3	5.4	5.4
NICs	9.5	13.9	15.0	17.3	19.3	19.3	19.2

NOTE: The figures for the European Community include only data for countries that were members before 1985. The newly industrializing countries (NICs) include Brazil, Hong Kong, Mexico, Singapore, South Korea, and Taiwan.
SOURCES: International Monetary Fund, *Direction of Trade Statistics*; and U.S. Department of Commerce, Bureau of the Census, *Highlights of U.S. Export and Import Trade*, FT990.

TABLE A–12

TOTAL U.S. EMPLOYMENT, BY SELECTED INDUSTRIES, 1980–1985
(thousands of workers)

Industry	1980	1981	1982	1983	1984	1985	1980–1985 (percent)
Total (millions)	99.3	100.4	99.5	100.8	105.0	107.2	7.9
Agriculture	3,366	3,372	3,406	3,381	3,325	3,187	−5.3
Construction	4,346	4,188	3,905	3,940	4,316	4,662	7.3
Mining	1,027	1,139	1,128	957	988	969	−5.6
Manufacturing	20,285	20,170	18,781	18,497	19,590	19,426	−4.2
Food and kindred products	1,708	1,671	1,635	1,622	1,643	1,637	−4.2
Tobacco manufactures	69	70	69	69	67	65	−5.7
Textile mill products	848	823	749	744	753	703	−17.1
Apparel products	1,264	1,244	1,161	1,164	1,202	1,162	−8.0
Lumber and wood products	691	666	598	658	710	703	1.8
Furniture and fixtures	466	464	432	447	484	497	6.7
Paper and allied products	693	689	662	662	682	683	−1.4
Printing and publishing	1,252	1,266	1,272	1,296	1,361	1,422	13.6
Chemical products	1,107	1,109	1,075	1,047	1,061	1,042	−5.9
Petroleum and coal products	198	214	201	195	188	177	−10.6
Rubber and plastic products	727	737	697	718	796	795	9.5
Leather products	233	238	219	208	202	175	−24.9
Stone, clay, and glass	662	638	577	573	605	600	−9.4
Primary metal products	1,142	1,122	922	838	874	816	−28.5

(Table continues)

85

TABLE A–12 (continued)

Industry	1980	1981	1982	1983	1984	1985	1980–1985 (percent)
Manufacturing (continued)							
Fabricated metal products	1,613	1,590	1,427	1,374	1,476	1,472	−8.7
Machinery, except electrical	2,494	2,498	2,244	2,038	2,214	2,181	−12.6
Electrical equipment	2,091	2,094	2,008	2,024	2,234	2,208	5.6
Transportation equipment	1,900	1,898	1,735	1,756	1,928	1,990	4.7
Instruments	711	730	716	695	723	724	1.8
Miscellaneous	418	408	382	371	387	376	−10.0
Transportation and public utilities	5,146	5,165	5,082	4,958	5,170	5,300	3.0
Wholesale trade	5,275	5,358	5,278	5,259	5,550	5,769	9.4
Retail trade	15,035	15,189	15,180	15,610	16,580	17,425	15.9
Finance, insurance, and real estate	5,160	5,300	5,340	5,470	5,680	5,924	14.8
Services	17,890	18,620	19,040	19,690	20,760	21,930	22.6

SOURCE: U.S. Department of Labor, Bureau of Labor Statistics, *Employment and Earnings*, various issues.

TABLE A-13
Structure of Total U.S. Employment, by Selected Industries, 1980–1985

Industry	1980	1981	1982	1983	1984	1985	1980–1985 (percent)
	Percentage of total U.S. employment						
Agriculture	3.4	3.4	3.4	3.4	3.2	3.0	−12.3
Construction	4.4	4.2	3.9	3.9	4.1	4.4	−0.6
Mining	1.0	1.1	1.1	0.9	0.9	0.9	−12.6
Manufacturing	20.4	20.1	18.9	18.3	18.7	18.1	−11.2
	Percentage of U.S. manufacturing employment						
Food and kindred products	8.4	8.3	8.7	8.8	8.4	8.4	0.1
Tobacco manufactures	0.3	0.3	0.4	0.4	0.3	0.3	−1.5
Textile mill products	4.2	4.1	4.0	4.0	3.8	3.6	−13.4
Apparel products	6.2	6.2	6.2	6.3	6.1	6.0	−4.0
Lumber and wood products	3.4	3.3	3.2	3.6	3.6	3.6	6.3
Furniture and fixtures	2.3	2.3	2.3	2.4	2.5	2.6	11.4
Paper and allied products	3.4	3.4	3.5	3.6	3.5	3.5	2.9
Printing and publishing	6.2	6.3	6.8	7.0	6.9	7.3	18.6
Chemical products	5.5	5.5	5.7	5.7	5.4	5.4	−1.7
Petroleum and coal products	1.0	1.1	1.1	1.1	1.0	0.9	−6.6
Rubber and plastic products	3.6	3.7	3.7	3.9	4.1	4.1	14.2
Leather products	1.1	1.2	1.2	1.1	1.0	0.9	−21.6
Stone, clay, and glass	3.3	3.2	3.2	3.1	3.1	3.1	−5.4

(Table continues)

87

TABLE A–13 (continued)

Industry	1980	1981	1982	1983	1984	1985	1980–1985 (percent)
Percentage of U.S. manufacturing employment							
Primary metal products	5.6	5.6	4.9	4.5	4.5	4.2	−25.4
Fabricated metal products	8.0	7.9	7.6	7.4	7.5	7.6	−4.7
Machinery, except electrical	12.3	12.4	11.9	11.0	11.3	11.2	−8.7
Electrical equipment	10.3	10.4	10.7	10.9	11.4	11.4	10.3
Transportation equipment	9.4	9.4	9.2	9.5	9.8	10.2	9.4
Instruments	3.5	3.6	3.8	3.8	3.7	3.7	6.3
Miscellaneous	2.1	2.0	2.0	2.0	2.0	1.9	−6.1
Percentage of total U.S. employment							
Transportation and public utilities	5.2	5.1	5.1	4.9	4.9	4.9	−4.5
Wholesale trade	5.3	5.3	5.3	5.2	5.3	5.4	1.4
Retail trade	15.1	15.1	15.3	15.5	15.8	16.3	7.4
Finance, insurance, and real estate	5.2	5.3	5.4	5.4	5.4	5.5	6.4
Services	18.0	18.5	19.1	19.5	19.8	20.5	13.5

SOURCE: U.S. Department of Labor, Bureau of Labor Statistics, *Employment and Earnings*, various issues.

TABLE A–14

U.S. REAL AVERAGE HOURLY EARNINGS, SELECTED INDUSTRIES, 1980–1985

(1972 dollars per hour)

Industry	1980	1981	1982	1983	1984	1985	1980–1985 (percent)
Total nonagriculture	3.62	3.59	3.57	3.60	3.59	3.58	−1.2
Construction	4.41	4.34	4.38	4.44	4.28	4.14	−6.1
Mining	1.74	1.46	1.62	1.79	1.85	1.91	9.7
Manufacturing	4.33	4.37	4.42	4.55	4.66	4.83	11.6
Food and kindred products	4.39	4.40	4.66	4.63	4.58	4.57	4.0
Tobacco manufactures	4.72	5.17	4.58	3.64	3.53	3.05	−35.3
Textile mill products	4.06	4.06	4.32	4.51	4.58	4.69	15.3
Apparel products	3.33	3.36	3.23	3.27	3.38	3.43	2.9
Lumber and wood products	3.99	4.29	4.15	3.84	3.99	4.14	3.6
Furniture and fixtures	3.44	3.39	3.32	3.39	3.44	3.36	−2.3
Paper and allied products	4.22	4.26	4.71	5.19	4.91	4.94	17.2
Printing and publishing	4.11	4.17	4.08	4.01	3.79	3.63	−11.8
Chemical products	5.13	5.12	5.57	5.94	6.12	6.16	20.1
Petroleum and coal products	4.94	4.53	3.85	3.48	3.51	3.40	−31.2
Rubber and plastic products	4.35	4.59	4.55	4.71	4.96	5.17	18.8
Leather products	2.54	2.60	2.69	2.78	3.01	2.88	13.2
Stone, clay, and glass	4.24	4.38	4.50	4.61	4.57	4.53	6.9
Primary metal products	4.51	4.60	5.00	4.93	4.82	5.06	12.2
Fabricated metal products	3.88	3.94	4.00	4.28	4.30	4.27	10.2

(Table continues)

TABLE A–14 (continued)

Industry	1980	1981	1982	1983	1984	1985	1980–1985 (percent)
Manufacturing (continued)							
Machinery, except electrial	4.55	4.69	4.80	5.68	6.34	7.57	66.5
Electrical equipment	5.10	5.18	5.26	5.45	5.58	5.77	13.2
Transportation equipment	6.44	6.11	5.88	5.98	6.11	6.20	–3.7
Instruments	4.50	4.54	4.66	4.76	4.86	5.02	11.6
Miscellaneous	2.55	2.73	2.85	2.94	3.12	3.22	26.3
Transportation and public utilities	5.22	5.16	4.99	4.91	4.85	4.74	–9.1
Wholesale trade	3.64	3.67	3.83	3.97	4.05	4.19	15.0
Retail trade	2.84	2.81	2.73	2.77	2.76	2.69	–5.2
Finance, insurance, and real estate	3.34	3.32	3.37	3.31	3.33	3.30	–1.1
Services	3.13	3.17	3.13	3.12	3.09	3.03	–3.1

NOTE: Average hourly earnings are for production and nonsupervisory workers and are deflated by implicit price deflator for that industry (real product wage).
SOURCE: U.S. Department of Labor, Bureau of Labor Statistics, *Employment and Earnings*, various issues.

TABLE A–15
U.S. Nominal Average Hourly Earnings, Selected Industries, 1980–1985
(dollars per hour)

Industry	1980	1981	1982	1983	1984	1985	1980–1985 (percent)
Total nonagriculture	6.66	7.25	7.68	8.02	8.33	8.58	28.8
Construction	9.94	10.80	11.62	11.94	12.12	12.26	23.6
Mining	9.16	10.02	10.79	11.28	11.63	11.96	30.6
Manufacturing	7.28	7.99	8.50	8.83	9.18	9.52	30.8
Food and kindred products	6.85	7.43	7.92	8.19	8.38	8.54	24.7
Tobacco manufactures	7.74	8.89	9.81	10.40	11.30	12.09	56.2
Textile mill products	5.08	5.52	5.83	6.18	6.46	6.70	31.9
Apparel products	4.56	4.97	5.20	5.37	5.55	5.72	25.4
Lumber and wood products	6.55	7.00	7.43	7.79	8.02	8.19	25.0
Furniture and fixtures	5.50	5.90	6.31	6.61	6.84	7.19	30.7
Paper and allied products	7.84	8.60	9.32	9.92	10.41	10.82	38.0
Printing and publishing	7.53	8.18	8.74	9.11	9.40	9.69	28.7
Chemical products	8.31	9.12	9.97	10.58	11.08	11.58	39.4
Petroleum and coal products	10.03	11.38	12.46	13.28	13.43	14.04	40.0
Rubber and plastic products	6.53	7.16	7.64	8.00	8.28	8.53	30.6
Leather products	4.58	4.99	5.33	5.54	5.71	5.82	27.1
Stone, clay, and glass	7.50	8.27	8.87	9.27	9.56	9.83	31.1
Primary metal products	9.78	10.81	11.34	11.35	11.47	11.68	19.4
Fabricated metal products	7.45	8.20	8.77	9.11	9.38	9.66	29.7

(Table continues)

TABLE A–15 (continued)

Industry	1980	1981	1982	1983	1984	1985	1980–1985 (percent)
Manufacturing (continued)							
Machinery, except electrical	8.00	8.81	9.26	9.55	9.96	10.29	28.6
Electrical equipment	6.94	7.62	8.21	8.66	9.04	9.47	36.5
Transportation equipment	9.34	10.39	11.12	11.66	12.21	12.71	36.1
Instruments	6.80	7.40	8.07	8.47	8.85	9.19	35.1
Miscellaneous	5.46	5.96	6.42	6.81	7.04	7.28	33.3
Transportation and public utilities	8.87	9.70	10.32	10.80	11.11	11.38	28.3
Wholesale trade	6.96	7.56	8.08	8.54	8.95	9.26	33.0
Retail trade	4.88	5.25	5.48	5.74	5.88	5.97	22.3
Finance, insurance, and real estate	5.78	6.31	6.78	7.29	7.62	7.93	37.2
Services	5.85	6.41	6.92	7.31	7.64	7.94	35.7

NOTE: Average hourly earnings are for production and nonsupervisory workers.
SOURCE: U.S. Department of Labor, Bureau of Labor Statistics, *Employment and Earnings,* various issues.

TABLE A–16

U.S. UNIT LABOR COST, SELECTED INDUSTRIES, 1980–1985

(Index, 1977 = 1.00)

Industry	1980	1981	1982	1983	1984	1985	1980–1985 (percent)
Total nonagriculture	1.27	1.37	1.48	1.51	1.53	1.56	23.0
Construction	1.41	1.63	1.71	1.69	1.73	1.86	31.8
Mining	1.55	1.83	2.07	1.93	1.94	1.99	28.2
Manufacturing	1.29	1.38	1.46	1.40	1.39	1.38	7.2
Food and kindred products	1.15	1.19	1.18	1.20	1.23	1.23	6.5
Tobacco manufactures	1.36	1.55	1.84	1.94	2.21	2.85	109.5
Textile mill products	1.14	1.22	1.25	1.17	1.25	1.28	13.0
Apparel products	1.12	1.20	1.25	1.23	1.25	1.32	17.3
Lumber and wood products	1.14	1.27	1.42	1.45	1.39	1.43	26.1
Furniture and fixtures	1.23	1.34	1.41	1.40	1.33	1.50	21.5
Paper and allied products	1.40	1.52	1.46	1.44	1.50	1.49	6.5
Printing and publishing	1.27	1.35	1.45	1.47	1.56	1.65	29.8
Chemical products	1.34	1.38	1.42	1.35	1.35	1.41	5.1
Petroleum and coal products	1.35	1.74	1.87	1.97	1.83	1.81	34.1
Rubber and plastic products	1.25	1.26	1.37	1.32	1.32	1.30	3.5
Leather and leather products	1.29	1.39	1.47	1.58	1.64	1.63	26.6
Stone, clay, and glass	1.28	1.46	1.54	1.47	1.43	1.46	13.4
Primary metal products	1.27	1.33	1.56	1.68	1.55	1.47	16.0
Fabricated metal products	1.23	1.35	1.46	1.38	1.39	1.44	16.7

(Table continues)

TABLE A–16 (continued)

Industry	1980	1981	1982	1983	1984	1985	1980–1985 (percent)
Manufacturing (continued)							
Machinery, except electrical	1.27	1.34	1.40	1.21	1.09	0.90	−29.4
Electrical equipment	1.13	1.22	1.31	1.30	1.36	1.34	18.3
Transportation equipment	1.53	1.82	1.93	1.65	1.61	1.70	10.7
Instruments	1.30	1.34	1.49	1.48	1.58	1.60	23.3
Miscellaneous	1.57	1.40	1.53	1.75	1.59	1.61	3.0
Transportation and public utilities	1.27	1.37	1.48	1.45	1.48	1.52	20.0
Wholesale trade	1.38	1.49	1.57	1.63	1.60	1.63	17.8
Retail trade	1.33	1.43	1.50	1.51	1.54	1.58	19.5
Finance, insurance, and real estate	1.32	1.45	1.57	1.67	1.76	1.84	39.7
Services	1.29	1.40	1.54	1.60	1.65	1.75	36.3

NOTE: Unit labor costs measure the labor cost required to produce one unit of output and are derived by dividing average hourly earnings by real output per hour.
SOURCES: U.S. Department of Commerce, Bureau of Economic Analysis, *National Income and Product Accounts;* and U.S. Department of Labor, Bureau of Labor Statistics, *Employment and Earnings,* various issues.

TABLE A-17

U.S. REAL OUTPUT, BY SELECTED INDUSTRIES, 1980–1985

(billions of 1972 dollars)

Industry	1980	1981	1982	1983	1984	1985	1980–1985 (percent)
Total	1,459	1,485	1,449	1,505	1,602	1,649	13.0
Agriculture	40.2	46.4	47.2	39.3	44.3	48.7	21.1
Construction	61.2	55.6	53.2	55.6	60.5	61.6	0.7
Mining	20.4	21.0	19.8	18.8	20.0	19.6	−3.9
Manufacturing	345.8	352.0	330.0	352.2	389.3	404.0	16.8
Food and kindred products	33.5	34.3	36.1	36.6	37.0	37.5	11.9
Tobacco manufactures	4.5	4.6	4.2	4.2	3.9	3.1	−31.1
Textile mill products	11.9	11.7	11.0	12.3	12.3	11.5	−3.4
Apparel products	12.5	12.6	11.7	12.4	13.0	12.3	−1.6
Lumber and wood products	11.4	10.5	8.9	10.1	11.7	11.5	0.9
Furniture and fixtures	5.4	5.3	5.0	5.4	6.4	6.2	14.8
Paper and allied products	12.4	12.4	13.5	14.6	15.1	15.8	27.4
Printing and publishing	17.3	18.0	17.9	18.7	19.2	19.4	12.1
Chemical products	28.1	29.9	30.9	33.5	35.5	35.1	24.9
Petroleum and coal products	8.3	7.9	7.5	7.4	7.7	7.7	−7.2
Rubber and plastic products	11.2	12.4	11.5	12.9	14.8	15.5	38.4
Leather products	2.2	2.2	2.1	1.9	1.8	1.6	−27.3
Stone, clay, and glass	10.7	10.1	9.2	10.0	11.2	11.2	4.7
Primary metal products	20.4	21.2	15.6	13.2	15.0	15.0	−26.5

(Table continues)

TABLE A–17 (continued)

Industry	1980	1981	1982	1983	1984	1985	1980–1985 (percent)
Manufacturing (continued)							
Fabricated metal products	24.0	23.8	21.1	22.3	24.6	24.3	1.3
Machinery, except electrical	43.7	45.9	41.5	44.8	56.6	69.6	59.3
Electrical equipment	40.4	41.3	39.6	42.6	47.0	49.3	22.0
Transportation equipment	37.9	35.4	32.6	40.6	47.9	48.7	28.5
Instruments	12.6	13.7	13.1	13.4	13.7	14.0	11.1
Miscellaneous	4.5	5.4	4.9	4.4	5.3	5.2	15.6
Transportation and public utilities	141.6	143.4	139.3	145.5	153.2	156.0	10.2
Wholesale trade	101.5	103.9	103.8	105.3	118.6	125.4	23.5
Retail trade	142.4	143.9	143.0	152.9	163.5	169.1	18.8
Finance, insurance, and real estate	231.6	236.5	236.4	243.8	252.0	261.1	12.7
Services	200.0	209.2	209.8	220.3	235.5	244.0	22.0

NOTE: Real output for each industry is derived by deflating the gross domestic product for that industry by its implicit price deflator. Detail may not add to totals because of rounding.
SOURCE: U.S. Department of Commerce, Bureau of Economic Analysis, *National Income and Product Accounts.*

TABLE A-18

U.S. NOMINAL OUTPUT, BY SELECTED INDUSTRIES, 1980–1985
(billions of dollars)

Industry	1980	1981	1982	1983	1984	1985	1980–1985 (percent)
Total	2,684	3,001	3,115	3,356	3,718	3,957	47.4
Agriculture	77.3	92.0	89.6	74.3	94.0	91.5	18.4
Construction	137.7	138.4	140.9	149.6	171.1	182.2	32.2
Mining	107.3	143.7	132.1	118.4	125.1	122.8	14.4
Manufacturing	581.0	643.1	634.6	683.2	766.9	795.8	37.0
Food and kindred products	52.2	57.9	61.4	64.7	67.7	70.2	34.5
Tobacco manufactures	7.3	7.9	8.9	11.9	12.4	12.4	69.9
Textile mill products	14.9	15.9	14.8	16.9	17.3	16.5	10.7
Apparel products	17.1	18.6	18.9	20.3	21.3	20.5	19.9
Lumber and wood products	18.7	17.1	16.0	20.5	23.6	22.8	21.9
Furniture and fixtures	8.6	9.2	9.5	10.6	12.8	13.2	53.5
Paper and allied products	23.0	25.1	26.7	27.8	32.1	34.6	50.4
Printing and publishing	31.6	35.2	38.4	42.4	47.5	51.9	64.2
Chemical products	45.5	53.3	55.3	59.6	64.3	65.9	44.8
Petroleum and coal products	16.8	19.8	24.4	28.3	29.6	31.9	89.9
Rubber and plastic products	16.8	19.3	19.3	21.9	24.7	25.5	51.8
Leather products	3.9	4.3	4.1	3.8	3.5	3.3	– 15.4
Stone, clay, and glass	19.0	19.0	18.2	20.2	23.4	24.4	28.4
Primary metal products	44.3	49.8	35.3	30.3	35.7	34.7	– 21.7

(Table continues)

TABLE A–18 (continued)

Industry	1980	1981	1982	1983	1984	1985	1980–1985 (percent)
Manufacturing (continued)							
Fabricated metal products	46.0	49.6	46.3	47.6	53.6	54.9	19.3
Machinery, except electrical	76.9	86.2	80.0	75.3	88.9	94.7	23.1
Electrical equipment	55.0	60.7	61.8	67.7	76.1	80.8	46.9
Transportation equipment	54.9	60.1	61.7	79.2	95.7	99.9	82.0
Instruments	19.0	22.3	22.6	23.9	24.9	25.7	35.3
Miscellaneous	9.6	11.7	11.1	10.3	11.9	11.8	22.9
Transportation and public utilities	240.8	269.6	288.4	320.0	350.9	374.4	55.5
Wholesale trade	193.9	214.0	219.0	226.5	262.1	277.2	43.0
Retail trade	245.0	269.1	287.5	316.4	348.3	375.3	53.2
Finance, insurance, and real estate	400.6	449.3	475.1	536.4	577.0	626.6	56.4
Services	374.0	422.6	463.6	515.5	581.6	639.4	71.0

SOURCE: U.S. Department of Commerce, Bureau of Economic Analysis, *National Income and Product Accounts.*

TABLE A-19
STRUCTURE OF U.S. REAL OUTPUT, 1980–1985

Industry	1980	1981	1982	1983	1984	1985	1980–1985 (percent)
Percentage of total U.S. output							
Agriculture	2.8	3.1	3.3	2.6	2.8	3.0	7.2
Construction	4.2	3.7	3.7	3.7	3.8	3.7	−11.0
Mining	1.4	1.4	1.4	1.3	1.2	1.2	−14.9
Manufacturing	23.7	23.7	22.8	23.4	24.3	24.5	3.4
Percentage of total U.S. manufacturing output							
Food and kindred products	9.7	9.7	10.9	10.4	9.5	9.3	−4.0
Tobacco manufactures	1.3	1.3	1.3	1.2	1.0	0.8	−39.8
Textile mill products	3.4	3.3	3.3	3.5	3.2	2.9	−17.1
Apparel products	3.6	3.6	3.6	3.5	3.3	3.0	−15.8
Lumber and wood products	3.3	3.0	2.7	2.9	3.0	2.9	−13.5
Furniture and fixtures	1.6	1.5	1.5	1.5	1.7	1.5	−1.8
Paper and allied products	3.6	3.5	4.1	4.1	3.9	3.9	9.4
Printing and publishing	5.0	5.1	5.4	5.3	4.9	4.8	−3.6
Chemical products	8.1	8.5	9.4	9.5	9.1	8.7	6.8
Petroleum and coal products	2.4	2.2	2.3	2.1	2.0	1.9	−20.1
Rubber and plastic products	3.2	3.5	3.5	3.7	3.8	3.8	18.1
Leather products	0.6	0.6	0.6	0.5	0.5	0.4	−35.4
Stone, clay, and glass	3.1	2.9	2.8	2.9	2.9	2.8	−10.3

(Table continues)

TABLE A–19 (continued)

Industry	1980	1981	1982	1983	1984	1985	1980–1985 (percent)
Percentage of total U.S. manufacturing output							
Primary metal products	5.9	6.0	4.7	3.7	3.9	3.7	−37.0
Fabricated metal products	6.9	6.8	6.4	6.3	6.3	6.0	−13.2
Machinery, except electrical	12.6	13.0	12.6	12.7	14.5	17.2	36.4
Electrical equipment	11.7	11.7	12.0	12.1	12.1	12.2	4.3
Transportation equipment	10.9	10.0	9.9	11.5	12.3	12.1	10.2
Instruments	3.6	3.9	4.0	3.8	3.5	3.5	−4.4
Miscellaneous	1.3	1.5	1.5	1.3	1.4	1.3	−0.4
Percentage of total U.S. output							
Transportation and public utilities	9.7	9.7	9.6	9.7	9.6	9.5	−2.5
Wholesale trade	7.0	7.0	7.2	7.0	7.4	7.6	9.3
Retail trade	9.8	9.7	9.9	10.2	10.2	10.3	5.0
Finance, insurance, and real estate	15.9	15.9	16.3	16.2	15.7	15.8	−0.2
Services	13.7	14.1	14.5	14.6	14.7	14.8	8.0

NOTE: Percentages may not add to 100.0 because of rounding.
SOURCE: U.S. Department of Commerce, Bureau of Economic Analysis, *National Income and Product Accounts*.

TABLE A-20

U.S. Real Output per Hour, Selected Industries, 1980–1985

(1972 dollars per hour)

Industry	1980	1981	1982	1983	1984	1985	1980–1985 (percent)
Total	7.06	7.11	7.00	7.18	7.34	7.40	4.8
Agriculture	5.74	6.61	6.66	5.59	6.41	7.34	27.9
Construction	6.77	6.38	6.55	6.79	6.73	6.35	-6.2
Mining	9.54	8.85	8.44	9.46	9.71	9.72	1.9
Manufacturing	8.20	8.39	8.45	9.15	9.55	10.00	22.0
Food and kindred products	9.42	9.86	10.61	10.83	10.82	11.03	17.1
Tobacco manufactures	31.06	31.37	29.10	29.20	27.89	23.16	-25.4
Textile mill products	6.76	6.83	7.03	7.98	7.84	7.89	16.7
Apparel products	4.75	4.86	4.86	5.11	5.20	5.08	6.9
Lumber and wood products	7.94	7.57	7.19	7.38	7.96	7.88	-0.8
Furniture and fixtures	5.55	5.47	5.56	5.85	6.38	5.97	7.6
Paper and allied products	8.58	8.68	9.79	10.58	10.67	11.12	29.6
Printing and publishing	6.63	6.82	6.78	6.93	6.76	6.57	-0.9
Chemical products	12.19	12.98	13.82	15.38	16.10	16.17	32.6
Petroleum and coal products	20.11	17.72	18.03	18.23	19.81	20.98	4.3
Rubber and plastic products	7.41	8.07	7.93	8.62	8.93	9.35	26.2
Leather products	4.47	4.52	4.55	4.41	4.38	4.49	0.4
Stone, clay, and glass	7.80	7.58	7.70	8.43	8.90	9.01	15.5

(Table continues)

101

TABLE A–20 (continued)

Industry	1980	1981	1982	1983	1984	1985	1980–1985 (percent)
Manufacturing (continued)							
Primary metal products	8.59	9.08	8.11	7.56	8.25	8.85	3.0
Fabricated metal products	7.14	7.21	7.12	7.82	8.01	7.93	11.1
Machinery, except electrical	8.42	8.82	8.88	10.57	12.29	15.35	82.3
Electrical equipment	9.30	9.48	9.48	10.11	10.11	10.73	15.4
Transportation equipment	9.58	8.96	9.05	11.12	11.93	11.77	22.9
Instruments	8.50	9.01	8.78	9.29	9.10	9.33	9.8
Miscellaneous	5.16	6.32	6.21	5.75	6.54	6.68	29.5
Transportation and public utilities	13.23	13.35	13.18	14.10	14.25	14.15	7.0
Wholesale trade	9.25	9.32	9.45	9.63	10.27	10.45	13.0
Retail trade	4.55	4.55	4.53	4.71	4.74	4.66	2.4
Finance, insurance, and real estate	21.58	21.45	21.28	21.43	21.33	21.19	−1.8
Services	5.37	5.40	5.30	5.38	5.45	5.35	−0.4

NOTE: Real output per hour is derived by dividing real gross domestic product by total employment for each sector. To calculate hourly output, the assumption of a forty-hour, fifty-two-week work year is made.
SOURCES: U.S. Department of Labor, Bureau of Labor Statistics, *Employment and Earnings*, various issues; and U.S. Department of Commerce, Bureau of Economic Analysis, *National Income and Product Accounts*.

TABLE A-21

U.S. REAL CORPORATE PROFITS, SELECTED INDUSTRIES, 1980–1985
(millions of 1972 dollars)

Industry	1980	1981	1982	1983	1984	1985	1980–1985 (percent)
Total	128,849	112,141	78,876	93,094	101,595	93,000	−27.8
Agriculture	467	274	105	6	−3	164	−64.8
Construction	2,923	1,801	1,183	1,274	1,149	820	−71.9
Mining	6,653	5,620	3,729	2,758	2,639	1,896	−71.5
Manufacturing	35,168	30,807	14,510	23,229	31,548	25,515	−27.4
Food and kindred products	4,724	4,417	4,021	4,362	3,972	3,744	−20.8
Tobacco manufactures	1,279	1,148	1,045	903	1,041	792	−38.0
Textile mill products	1,135	890	496	1,099	776	174	−84.7
Apparel products	1,455	1,533	1,454	1,840	1,597	1,131	−22.3
Lumber and wood products	812	−322	−254	1,028	1,486	1,224	50.8
Furniture and fixtures	627	606	664	724	1,085	857	36.7
Paper and allied products	1,944	1,681	1,751	1,691	2,175	1,939	−0.2
Printing and publishing	2,574	2,474	2,187	2,514	2,789	2,764	7.4
Chemical products	4,357	4,721	2,439	3,560	3,833	1,926	−55.8
Petroleum and coal products	706	−232	7	−145	−466	−357	−150.6
Rubber and plastic products	450	1,000	854	1,264	1,274	852	89.2
Leather products	392	351	319	234	135	149	−62.1
Stone, clay, and glass	787	168	−171	470	1,177	1,329	68.9

(Table continues)

TABLE A–21 (continued)

Industry	1980	1981	1982	1983	1984	1985	1980–1985 (percent)
Manufacturing (continued)							
Primary metal products	1,517	1,272	−2,920	−3,322	−2,468	−2,829	−286.5
Fabricated metal products	3,236	3,389	1,700	1,938	2,618	2,052	−36.6
Machinery, except electrical	5,788	5,620	2,098	368	1,383	903	−84.4
Electrical equipment	4,396	3,633	1,322	2,133	2,467	2,677	−39.1
Transportation equipment	−4,043	−3,845	−2,771	3,569	6,611	4,699	216.2
Instruments	1,988	1,907	840	666	735	667	−66.5
Miscellaneous	686	780	588	−76	269	353	−48.5
Transportation and public utilities	12,352	11,330	10,143	13,332	14,774	13,480	9.1
Wholesale trade	17,462	16,064	12,748	14,663	17,222	16,112	−7.7
Retail trade	7,849	7,818	8,658	10,237	10,545	10,714	36.5
Finance, insurance, and real estate	13,273	8,955	4,648	7,984	6,866	8,980	−32.3
Services	5,517	6,015	4,879	5,089	5,121	5,008	−9.2

NOTE: Corporate profits are deflated by implicit price deflator for that industry.
SOURCE: U.S. Department of Commerce, Bureau of Economic Analysis, *National Income and Product Accounts*.

Appendix B
Domestic Savings and Investment and the Current Account

The relationship between a country's domestic macroeconomic imbalance and its current account can be derived from GNP accounting identities and set out in the following equation:

$$PS + GS - I = CA$$

$PS + GS$	I	CA
Domestic savings	Domestic investment	Current or capital account

where PS = gross private domestic savings (the sum of corporate and household savings); GS = general government budget surplus or deficit (the sum of the central, state, and local government budget surpluses or deficits); I = gross private domestic investment; and CA = current or capital account (the current account, the sum of the balance on trade in goods plus the balance on services, interest, and transfers, equals the capital account, net foreign investment).

When domestic savings (private savings plus the budget surplus or deficit) fall short of the demand for savings (gross private investment), the imbalance is made up by the inflow of foreign funds, the capital account. That is, if domestic demand for output is greater than the supply of domestic output, the excess demand is satisfied by foreign output, creating a current account deficit. From either viewpoint, the capital account or current account offsets the domestic macroeconomic imbalance. Without these offsetting movements the domestic demand for savings or output must be reduced. Similarly, if policy acts to reduce these foreign flows of funds, domestic demand will suffer.

The following table illustrates the macroeconomic imbalances of the major industrial countries for 1983, in billions of U.S. dollars.

	GS + PS	−	I	=	CA
United States	− 124 + 622	−	533	=	− 34
Japan	35 + 317	−	331	=	21
United Kingdom	− 2 + 85	−	79	=	4
Germany	10 + 133	−	138	=	5
France	2 + 92	−	102	=	− 8

NOTE: Detail may not add to totals because of rounding.
SOURCES: OECD, National Income Accounts; and IMF, *International Financial Statistics*.

Appendix C
Real Exchange Rates for
Various Commodities

The appreciation of the dollar was broadly based and took place against the majority of America's trading partners. The broad nature of the dollar's appreciation was felt economy-wide, as discussed in chapter 2, with most products feeling the adverse effects of the dollar's rise.

Figure C–1 shows the bilateral nominal exchange rate between the dollar and a diverse selection of currencies. From these nominal exchange rates real exchange rates for a variety of product groups have been calculated (figures C–2 to C–10). These real rates were derived by adjusting the nominal exchange rates for relative movements in prices—in these cases for the relative differences in hourly compensation.

It is impressive to note the difference between the nominal and real exchange rates. The steeper rise in the real yen-dollar rate suggests that hourly compensation for the majority of products shown here rose faster in the United States than in Japan. The large nominal depreciation of the Korean won against the dollar, however, is offset to a large extent by the faster growth of Korean hourly compensation.

The real exchange rates presented in the figures of this appendix underscore the broad-based deterioration of U.S. competitiveness in the 1980s. These figures present convincing evidence that the exchange rate played a key role in the competitive difficulties encountered by American exporters and producers of import-competing products. But as we demonstrated in chapter 2, the exchange rates did not start to appreciate without cause in the early 1980s. The explanation for the dramatic change in exchange rates and in U.S. competitiveness has to rest with macroeconomic policies and imbalances in the United States.

FIGURE C–1

U.S. NOMINAL EXCHANGE RATES, 1975–1986
(1975 = 1.00)

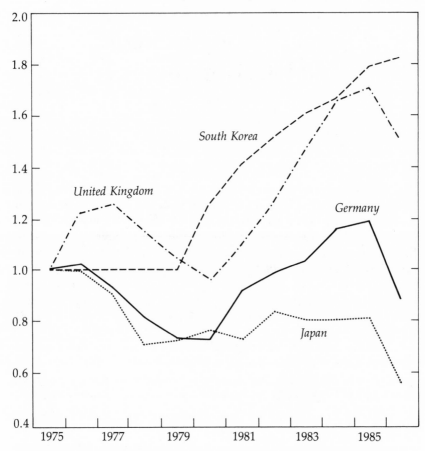

NOTE: Nominal exchange rates are measured in foreign currency per U.S. dollar.
SOURCE: International Monetary Fund, *International Financial Statistics*.

FIGURE C–2

U.S. REAL EXCHANGE RATES, ALL MANUFACTURING PRODUCTS, 1975–1986
(1975 = 1.00)

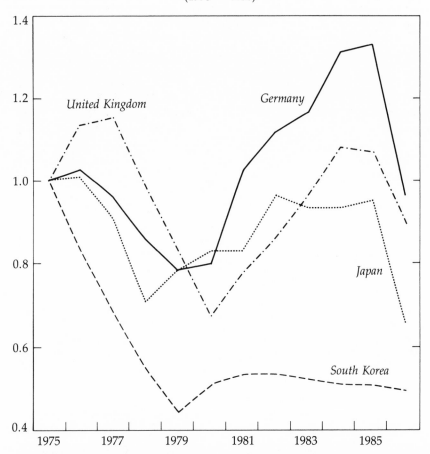

NOTE: The real exchange rate, based on the authors' calculations, is defined as the American price level divided by the partner country's price level multiplied by the nominal exchange rate, in this case, $(W/W^*)\,(E)$, where E is the nominal exchange rate and W^* and W are foreign and domestic hourly compensation respectively for all manufacturing products.
SOURCE: International Monetary Fund, *International Financial Statistics*.

FIGURE C–3

U.S. REAL EXCHANGE RATES, TEXTILE MILL PRODUCTS, 1975–1985
(1975 = 1.0)

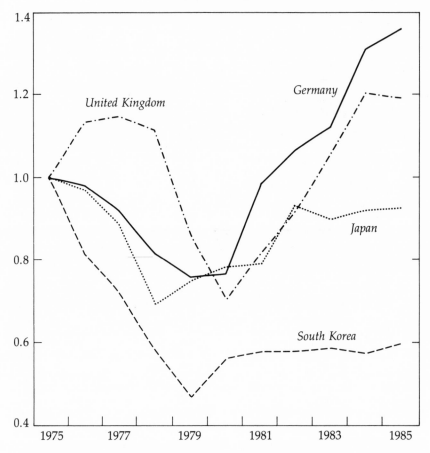

NOTE: The real exchange rate, based on the authors' calculations, is defined as the American price level divided by the partner country's price level multiplied by the nominal exchange rate, in this case, (W/W^*) (E), where E is the nominal exchange rate and W^* and W are foreign and domestic hourly compensation respectively for textile mill products.

SOURCE: International Monetary Fund, *International Financial Statistics*.

FIGURE C-4

U.S. REAL EXCHANGE RATES, APPAREL PRODUCTS, 1975–1985
(1975 = 1.0)

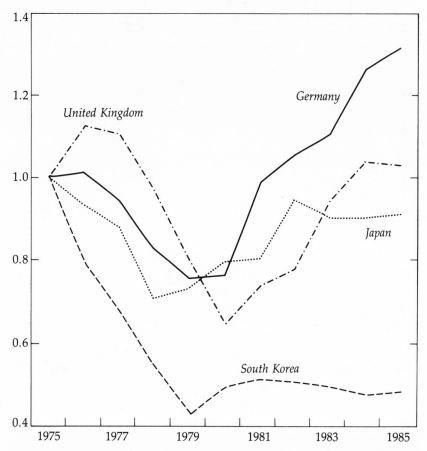

NOTE: The real exchange rate, based on the authors' calculations, is defined as the American price level divided by the partner country's price level multiplied by the nominal exchange rate, in this case, (W/W^*) (E), where E is the nominal exchange rate and W^* and W are foreign and domestic hourly compensation respectively for apparel products.

SOURCE: International Monetary Fund, *International Financial Statistics*.

FIGURE C–5

U.S. Real Exchange Rates, Chemicals and Allied Products,
1975–1985
(1975 = 1.0)

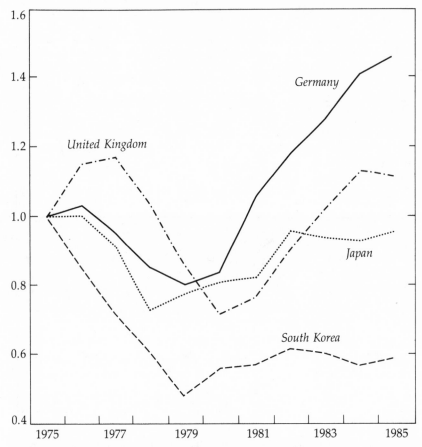

NOTE: The real exchange rate, based on the authors' calculations, is defined as the American price level divided by the partner country's price level multiplied by the nominal exchange rate, in this case, (W/W^*) (E), where E is the nominal exchange rate and W^* and W are foreign and domestic hourly compensation respectively for chemicals and allied products.
SOURCE: International Monetary Fund, *International Financial Statistics*.

FIGURE C–6

U.S. REAL EXCHANGE RATES, IRON AND STEEL PRODUCTS, 1975–1986
(1975 = 1.0)

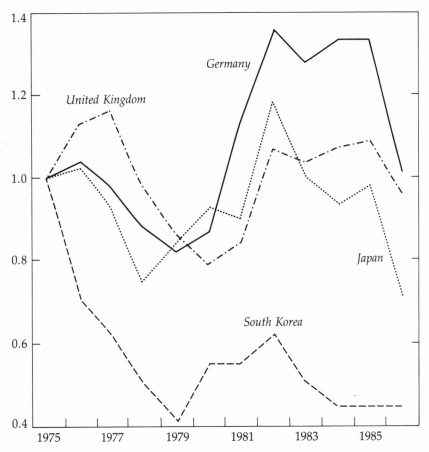

NOTE: The real exchange rate, based on the authors' calculations, is defined as the American price level divided by the partner country's price level multiplied by the nominal exchange rate, in this case, $(W/W^*)\ (E)$, where E is the nominal exchange rate and W^* and W are foreign and domestic hourly compensation respectively for iron and steel products.
SOURCE: International Monetary Fund, *International Financial Statistics*.

FIGURE C–7

U.S. REAL EXCHANGE RATES, MACHINERY, EXCEPT ELECTRICAL, 1975–1985
(1975 = 1.0)

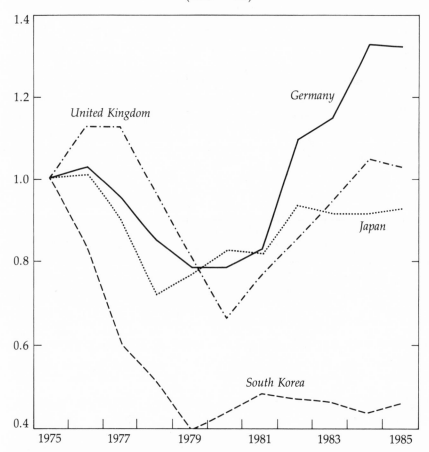

NOTE: The real exchange rate, based on the authors' calculations, is defined as the American price level divided by the partner country's price level multiplied by the nominal exchange rate, in this case, (W/W^*) (E), where E is the nominal exchange rate and W^* and W are foreign and domestic hourly compensation respectively for machinery, except electrical products.

SOURCE: International Monetary Fund, *International Financial Statistics*.

FIGURE C–8

U.S. REAL EXCHANGE RATES, ELECTRIC AND ELECTRONIC EQUIPMENT, 1975–1985
(1975 = 1.0)

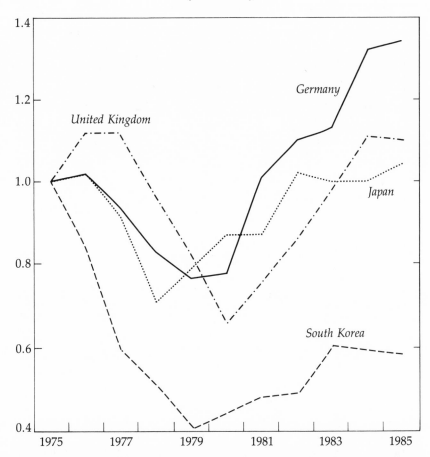

NOTE: The real exchange rate, based on the authors' calculations, is defined as the American price level divided by the partner country's price level multiplied by the nominal exchange rate, in this case, (W/W^*) (E), where E is the nominal exchange rate and W^* and W are foreign and domestic hourly compensation respectively for electric and electronic equipment.
SOURCE: International Monetary Fund, *International Financial Statistics.*

FIGURE C–9

U.S. REAL EXCHANGE RATES, MOTOR VEHICLES AND EQUIPMENT, 1975–1986
(1975 = 1.0)

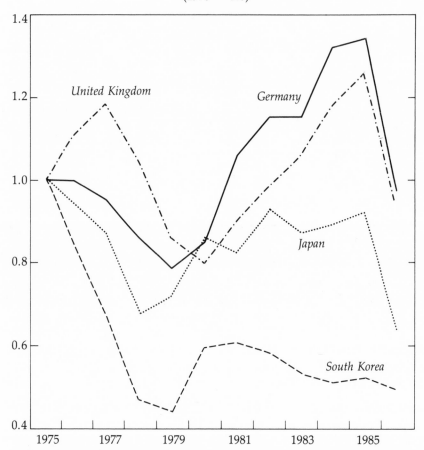

NOTE: The real exchange rate, based on the authors' calculations, is defined as the American price level divided by the partner country's price level multiplied by the nominal exchange rate, in this case, (W/W^*) (E), where E is the nominal exchange rate and W^* and W are foreign and domestic hourly compensation respectively for motor vehicles and equipment.
SOURCE: International Monetary Fund, *International Financial Statistics*.

FIGURE C–10

U.S. REAL EXCHANGE RATES, INSTRUMENTS AND RELATED PRODUCTS, 1975–1985
(1975 = 1.0)

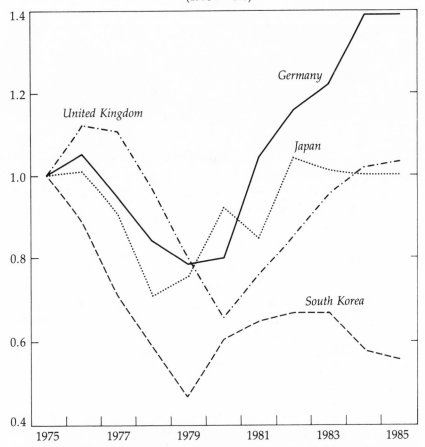

NOTE: The real exchange rate, based on the authors' calculations, is defined as the American price level divided by the partner country's price level multiplied by the nominal exchange rate, in this case, (W/W^*) (E), where E is the nominal exchange rate and W^* and W are foreign and domestic hourly compensation respectively for instruments and related products.

SOURCE: International Monetary Fund, *International Financial Statistics*.

Appendix D
How Many Trade Balances
Are There?

What is the size of the U.S. trade deficit? Most newspapers reported that in 1986 the United States had another record-breaking deficit of $169.8 billion. The Department of Commerce agreed that 1986 set a new record for the trade deficit but reported in its National Income and Product Accounts a figure of $147.7 billion. To confuse things even more, most economists refer to the sum of $140.6 billion when describing the record-breaking trade deficit of 1986.

Which one of these trade deficit figures is correct? Is the trade deficit $169.8 billion, $147.7 billion, or $140.6 billion? Oddly enough, each figure is correct. There is no chicanery involved, only a bit of definitional looseness in the term "trade deficit." These trade deficits differ in size because of the way in which they are reported and measured. What the newspapers are referring to is more correctly known as the merchandise trade deficit. Unfortunately, this merchandise trade deficit can itself be measured and reported in several ways. The Department of Commerce will report in some of its publications the trade deficit as it is defined in the U.S. National Income and Product Accounts. The most comprehensive definition of the trade deficit, though not necessarily the largest figure, is supplied under the heading of the current account deficit.

Each of these trade deficits is meant to be used for a specific purpose. More often than not they are misused. For that reason the various definitions are summarized in this appendix.

The Current Account

The current account, being the most comprehensive summary of the U.S. trade position, includes all the items mentioned in the other definitions of the trade deficit or surplus. Simply put, it is the sum of the balance on trade in goods (merchandise trade), the balance on trade in services, and unilateral transfers.

The current account deficit will differ from the merchandise trade deficit as long as the balance on trade in services and unilateral transfers is not zero. The United States has historically run a surplus on the service component of the current account; thus the current account figures have been in surplus at times when the merchandise trade balance was in deficit. In the 1980s, as the merchandise trade balance plunged to repeated record deficits and the surplus on the service component shrank, the distinction between the size of the current account and the merchandise trade balance became less pronounced.

As mentioned in chapter 2, when U.S. demand for goods and services is not met by domestic suppliers, that demand is met by running a current account deficit—the net import of goods and services from abroad. The importance of the current account deficit is that it is also a measure of the net amount the United States borrows from abroad to finance its excess domestic demand. The capital account—the net sale of financial or real assets—must by the nature of double-entry bookkeeping mirror the current account. Thus last year the United States ran a current account deficit of $140.6 billion; it consumed $140.6 billion more than it produced. Alternatively, the United States borrowed a net amount of $140.6 billion from abroad; foreigners acquired an additional $140.6 billion in claims against the future production of the United States.

The Merchandise Trade Balance

The most sizable component of the current account deficit is the merchandise trade balance. It measures the net export of all tangible commodities, such as cars, radios, wheat, and steel. It differs from the current account in that it excludes trade in services. If the trade balance in services is large, the merchandise trade balance is not an accurate reflection of the net amount of financing obtained from abroad.

Merchandise trade figures are reported several ways, depending on the extent to which the various services involved in transportation are included. Exports and imports measured on a free alongside ship (f.a.s.) basis reflect the transaction value of goods delivered to the point of departure, ready for shipment to or from the United States. The f.a.s. valuation excludes items such as loading cost and insurance and thus is the closest measure of the value of the goods themselves. U.S. exports are usually reported on this basis, but U.S. imports are not. Export and import figures can also be measured on a free on board (f.o.b.) basis. In addition to the value of the goods, the f.o.b.

valuation includes loading and related costs. The addition of insurance and freight results in yet another measure of exports and imports, the cost, insurance, and freight (c.i.f.) basis. U.S. imports are reported on a c.i.f. basis but are most often measured on a customs valuation basis. Methodologically, the customs value is similar to the f.a.s. basis in determining the value of the product at the point of origin, that is, exclusive of loading, insurance, freight, and related costs. The difference is that the U.S. Customs Service, not the importer or exporter, determines the value of the product.

As shown in table D–1, the method of valuation of exports and imports can result in very different trade figures. U.S. publications on exports and imports have changed the valuation basis for reporting export and import figures several times over the years. They now prefer to report exports on an f.a.s. basis and imports on a c.i.f. and customs value basis.

TABLE D–1

EXPORTS AND IMPORTS UNDER VARIOUS VALUATION METHODS, 1985
(billions of U.S. dollars)

	f.a.s.	f.o.b.	c.i.f.	Customs Value
Exports	206.9	213.2	—	—
Imports	—	338.9	361.6	345.3

f.a.s. = free alongside ship; f.o.b. = free on board; c.i.f. = cost, insurance, and freight.